COLOR IN DECORATION

by JOSE WILSON and ARTHUR LEAMAN, A.I.D.

VNR Van Nostrand Reinhold Company / New York

Studio Vista Limited / London

Van Nostrand Reinhold Company Regional Offices:
New York   Cincinnati   Chicago   Millbrae   Dallas

Van Nostrand Reinhold Company International Offices:
London   Toronto   Melbourne

Library of Congress Catalog Card Number: 79-90332

Designed by Jacqueline Brunet
Drawings by Jane Geayer

Published by Van Nostrand Reinhold Company,
A Division of Litton Educational Publishing, Inc.,
450 West 33rd Street, New York, N. Y. 10001

Published simultaneously in Canada by
Van Nostrand Reinhold Ltd.

Published in Great Britain
by Studio Vista
Blue Star House, Highgate Hill, London N19

SBN 289 70220 8

3   5   7   9   11   13   15   16   14   12   10   8   6   4   2

CONTENTS

Preface   7

The Continuity of Color 1   8

The Combinations of Color 2   18

Color at Work 3   32

The Color Environment 4   60

Light and Color 5   78

Color on the Outside 6   88

The Language of Color 7   101

Bibliography   159

For their help in compiling material for this book

the authors thank the following magazines:

ANTIQUES

HOUSE & GARDEN

HOUSE BEAUTIFUL

INTERIORS

INTERIOR DESIGN

LADIES' HOME JOURNAL

and Barbara Lennox, Los Angeles, California

Preface

This is a good book on its subject, and a unique one. Most publishers feel the need for works on interior decoration, the subject being one of universal interest. Yet so many are mere picture books basted with trivial legends and the academic repetition of outmoded ideas. I have a wide shelf of them and doubt if I have read more than a few lines in any. The pictures are what have counted, and even these often tend to be outmoded as well.

A book on Color in Decoration *comes at the right time. More and more the art of home design relies on it. Even the popular all-white interior (which thankfully has seen its day) would be sterile like a hospital or bleak like a snowscape if it weren't for the infusion of color accents placed within it. In the process of vision, which involves the eye, brain and human psyche itself, color and brightness take precedence over form and design. Color is the first impression to register in consciousness. A wall is a wall or a sofa a sofa; they take on character and spirit only when colored. A dozen white sofas in a dozen different forms would be far less engaging than the same sofa in a dozen different colors. And the colors would be better remembered than the forms.*

A book on color and decoration meant to be read for its text as well as seen for its illustrations is perhaps something of a novelty. Being an old hand at color, I congratulate José Wilson and Arthur Leaman for getting me to relish type matter as well as picture. I have learned much. Best of all, I have been treated to refreshingly new and original viewpoints. Now I am all set to redo an apartment of mine in ways that would not otherwise have dawned on me.

I admire the generous credit given to leading designers of the day. I like the blithe style of writing which swings along on an energetic vocabulary and never drags. A glossary on the Language of Color in Decoration is the best I have yet encountered.

But what has impressed me most is the awareness of the authors of changes taking place in modern modes of living. While tradition will still be revered—though pepped up a bit with contemporary colors—life in the future will be spent less in nature than in contrived spaces. Here emphasis on light and illumination as decorative functions, computer-controlled colored lighting effects, lumia projections to replace or supplement static works of art, innovations everywhere, in furniture, graphics, materials, all are in this excellent book.

As a champion of color, I hope Wilson and Leaman are right and prophetic in what they forecast. I feel pretty sure they are.

Faber Birren

THE CONTINUITY OF COLOR

The history of decoration might start with the words, "In the beginning there was color." No matter how spare, almost nonexistent the decoration and furnishing of houses and rooms, color was the one constant, the leitmotif that expressed the moods and mores of the times, the life domestic, and the innate desire in human beings to leave their mark on their surroundings and render them more beautiful and personal. Throughout history, color in decoration has faithfully mirrored the period—its spirit, its fashions, its preoccupations and its manners. Grandiloquent epochs like the French Empire and the Victorian were characterized by intense, dark colors—reds and blues, purples and greens. The eighteenth-century ages of wit and reason preferred softer colors, elegant and reflective, sophisticatedly paled and neutralized. In the ancient civilizations, the symbolism of color was more important than its decorative value. Theirs were the strong, clear primaries and secondaries whose use was codified. It was not until the Renaissance that color was used for its own sake. Colors became more complex, neutralized, richer and more sensuous, emblazoned with gold. New pigments were invented to augment the limited number of dyes.

Although every period can lay claim to its own color schemes, colors tend to run in cycles. There is a perennial outcropping of traditional color combinations, updated and handled in new ways. The main difference between the decoration of today and that of the past—for there are many similarities—is the fantastic range of synthetic dyes and pigments we have at our disposal, permitting more gradations and subtleties in our color schemes. We also live in an age where, because of rapid communications, we have more turnover of colors, more trends and overnight sensations and, as never before, continual experimentation with color for color's sake.

Frescoes of false architecture in sparsely furnished Pompeian rooms set the precedent for the trompe l'oeil background, *top*. Courtesy The Metropolitan Museum of Art, Rogers Fund, 1903.

Stylized mural by Ralph Adron inundates old-fashioned bathroom of designer Max Clendinning with Surrealist images, swirling patterns and colors, *right*. Photograph by Michael Boys.

Projected background, today's trompe l'oeil, was used by interior designer C. Ray Smith to add a changeable element of fantasy to a white living room, *far right*. Photograph by Louis Reens.

Among the basic influences that have created decorative styles in different periods, climatic conditions and available materials rank high. How these influences operate in countries and centuries far apart is shown here. In both cases, light diffused through a translucent material colored in bright clear tones (glass in eighteenth-century India, plastic in twentieth-century America) irradiates a neutral interior while screening out the heat and intensity of strong sun.

Stained glass, an early form of architectural decoration that marries color and light, makes a glorious, glowing background for a starkly furnished black-and-white marble bedroom in the eighteenth-century Jag Nivas at Udaipur, now the Lake Palace Hotel. Photograph by Fotiades.

Brilliant sheets of stock acrylic plastic recreate the effect of costly stained glass in a summer pavilion designed by Mallory-Tillis, A.I.D. Paisley-patterned fabric, wood-and-grape-vine étagère introduce a sense of Eastern exoticism. Photograph by Grigsby. Courtesy American Cyanamid.

Classic blue-and-white color scheme, reinterpreted in the modern idiom by Michael Taylor,
A.I.D., silhouettes brilliant cornflower-blue upholstery against an all-white background,
mingles blue and white in old Delft jars, china and flowers. Photograph by Fred Lyon.

Traditional version of the blue-and-white look decorates the walls of the early eighteenth-
century dining room in the Château de Rambouillet with Delft tiles. Polychrome panels of urns,
bouquets are set in like paintings. Photograph by J. Guillot. Courtesy Connaissance des Arts.

A similar red-and-purple color scheme handled in a crisp, contemporary way by interior designer Harold Imber pits concentrated slabs of color in upholstery and a fabric wall panel against a light background, with pattern confined to the sofa. Photograph by Grigsby. Courtesy House & Garden.

The rich patterns and luxurious textures that characterized French style in the 1880's are reassembled in the Comte de R's Paris apartment. Color is lavished on walls and floor—Aubusson tapestry and rug, red portières, green moiré papier-peint. Photograph by R. Bonnefoy. Courtesy Connaissance des Arts.

Historical precedents prove that as far as color in decoration is concerned, there is nothing new under the sun. All that has changed is the manner in which it is used. Past centuries had craftsmen who could spend unlimited time and care on carved and inlaid furniture, wood paneling, mosaic and parquet floors, hand-painted wallpapers and handwoven tapestries. We have, of necessity, speeded up and simplified the logistics of decoration, producing materials that simulate the old craftsmanship, processes that enable us to get the same effects at a fraction of the cost. It is enlightening to see how differently today's interior designers deal with traditional color schemes. Instead of using color wholesale around a room for a total look, they distribute it in specific sharp doses where it can have the most impact—in furniture, fabrics, accessories, on a floor or one wall and, more and more, in huge, dominant modern paintings. The rooms opposite show the changes that have taken place in two of the longest-lasting decorative uses of color: painted furniture and painted walls. Eighteenth-century painted furniture was a work of art and was encased like a jewel in a setting of comparable elegance. We treat painted furniture as a punctuation point of color, rather than as an integral part of a room scheme. The painted background has undergone an even greater transition. The pastel boiserie of eighteenth-century France, with its exquisite overpainted panels, has given way to bolder wall colors and, in small areas, clashing color contrasts between art and background. Our approach has been much influenced by contemporary art, which breaks down the barriers of convention. Ours is, perhaps, a new Renaissance, the first age to embrace technology wholeheartedly and use it properly as an aid to unfettered self-expression.

17

THE COMBINATIONS OF COLOR

The words employed by professionals to express the mystique and workings of color often sound more complicated than they are. Monochromatic, analogous, complementary, split-complementary, analogous-complementary, triadic, are technical terms that describe combinations taken from the color wheel, the device on which the majority of decorating schemes are based. It was Sir Isaac Newton, he of apple-and-gravity fame, who first classified the colors of the wheel, in the order they appeared when light was refracted through a prism. While he listed seven colors (red, yellow, orange, blue, green, purple and indigo), the color wheel we use has just six, composed of the primaries (red, blue and yellow) and the secondaries (orange, green and purple), further extended by the in-between tertiaries, which result from mixing the primaries and secondaries.

Later systems devised by Albert H. Munsell and Wilhelm Ostwald were much more complex and are mainly utilized by manufacturers and others who wish to classify colors more technically and finitely. In these systems, colors are grouped in a three-dimensional solid and rated by letter and number according to their hue, value and chroma, or the proportions of pure color, black and white. A less bewildering system, proposed by colorist Faber Birren, is composed of a circle of twelve lettered hues with nine numbered steps ranging from black (the shades) to white (the tints). Such devices are better seen than described. Their main purpose and value is to enable a color to be identified by an exact notation, rather than by a vaguely associative name such as sky blue, leaf green or carnation pink, and to provide exact formulas which may be used internationally by paint companies and dye manufacturers. Where such pinpointing is vital, they work extremely well; but for the everyday objectives of decorating, it is usually sufficient to master the principles of the color wheel and the role of black and white in producing shades or tints of the pure hue. (A fuller explanation of such words as tint, shade, value and chroma will be found in the final chapter.) From this it is possible to plan color schemes based on the primaries, secondaries, tertiaries and neutrals. As a beginning, take white, a no-color that is actually the combination of all the colors in the rainbow, or spectral colors. The all-white room, infinitively receptive to color accents, finds its total expression in the clean-lined, hard-edge room opposite.

A decorating perennial, the all-white room, undergoes periodic changes that bring it into line with current trends. In the mood of the seventies, this huge, wide-open living room designed by Richard Himmel, A.I.D., is as stark and primed for color accents as the snowscape beyond the windows. Dead-white walls, floor and sofas silhouette bold patterns and strong shapes. Photograph by Idaka.

Once white was strictly for the wealthy, who could afford the impracticality of satin and silk, damask and brocade. Now, reinterpreted in paint, plastics, synthetics and substitutes, it is for everyone. Next to white, the simplest color scheme to handle is the monochromatic—different values of one color family, usually grounded with black or dark neutrals or lightened by lashings of white or pale neutrals, like the in-the-pink room on the opposite page.

Analogous refers to colors that are neighbors on the color wheel and therefore have something in common—blue and green on the cool side of the spectrum, yellow and orange in the warm range. This is one of the easiest formulas for putting two colors together, although there are some provisos—an analogous scheme should always contain more of one color than the other, for an equal balance of such close cousins would mean they canceled each other out. Warm colors, such as yellow and orange, also require the relief of deep tones, such as dark woods, to provide ballast for their buoyancy; and blue and green welcome the brilliance of reflected light from steel, mirror, glossy white vinyl. An accent of blue (the complement of orange) is all it takes to turn an orange-and-yellow analogous color scheme into analogous-complementary. Like every scheme, the analogous complementary admits of different treatments. Many traditional rooms are done in this way, but the colors are muted—tints and shades rather than primaries and secondaries—and distributed around the room in small, discreet amounts. It might, in fact, be said that the mark of present-day decorating, as opposed to that of the past, is the unabashed, uninhibited use of strong colors over large areas.

Even decorous Colonial interiors can benefit from a kind of decorating shock treatment. Whereas ten years ago it might have been considered heresy to base a complementary color scheme on conspicuous proportions of blue and yellow or red and green as we would today, it is master strokes like this that have the power to update dull or outmoded architecture.

Possibly the most difficult of all color schemes to work with is the triadic, in which three colors equidistant on the wheel (red, yellow and blue for example) are combined. Unless they are carefully and properly balanced, the result can be as garishly jumpy as a circus poster. One of the best ways to handle a triadic scheme is first to pick a print that combines all three colors, then choose one to predominate on a large area—walls or floor—and use the others as accents.

Color schemes don't just happen. They either derive from the past and are interpreted in new ways—the case with the ever-popular blue-and-white look shown in eighteenth- and twentieth-century guises on pages 12 and 13, or they spring like thunderbolts from the daring of a designer of interiors, stage sets or fashions. Initially met with disdain or derision, in a matter of a few years they find their way to public acceptance on a mass-market level. When you consider how orthodox a blue-and-green color scheme seems these days, it is difficult to believe that less than twenty years ago it was regarded as just about the most outrageous and avant-garde thing going. Melanie Kahane first introduced the combination of pink and orange, but it took a successful musical, "The King and I," with its fantastic rainbow costumes of bright, hot Siamese pinks and oranges to popularize a then startling color team. Neutrals took a great step forward with Cecil Beaton's Ascot finale in "My Fair Lady." Now it is the turn of the leading names in couture, such as Emilio Pucci, to move into the home furnishings field with individual, compelling fusions of color and pattern. Artists have always had a subtly undermining influence on hidebound concepts of what color looks right with what, but it has taken the luminescent, pulsating, psychedelic combinations favored by the young finally to break into the bastion of the middle-class home. Color cycles come faster now, burn out quicker. Spearheading the trends and keeping a canny finger on the pulse of public taste are House & Garden—and Faber Birren, consultant for the magazine's Color Program—and House Beautiful. It all adds up to a staggering turnover in color styles and trends that makes this year's hit old hat next year.

Subtle interpretation of a modern analogous color scheme of apricot and gold exploits the rich textures of silk and velvet. The soft, opulent materials bring a sense of eighteenth-century luxe to a traditional sitting room designed by Burge-Donghia, A.I.D., N.S.I.D. Photograph by Hans Van Nes.

The practice of changing the color scheme or the seasonal aspect of a room with accessories is undoubtedly one of the most fundamental characteristics of twentieth-century decoration. Although most of these accessories—pillows and lamps, vases and ashtrays, accent rugs and screens—have a practical purpose, function usually comes second to form in their selection. They are chosen first with an eye to their color and shape, the part they will play in the overall setting, rather than their ability to cushion a chair, cover a floor, hold an arrangement of flowers or light a corner. This purely modern concept of accessories (which may be loosely defined as the changeable, decorative elements in a room, as distinct from the major furnishings) has no antecedent in the past. The pottery and porcelains, scrolls, screens and tapestries of the ancient Greeks and Romans, the Chinese, the Italians of the Renaissance and the eighteenth-century French and English were valued for their functional or esthetic qualities, independent of their background. Ours is the age when "decorative accessories" spell big business. In the well-decorated room, everything has a place and everything must fit in, which is the reason why so often the accessories are more expensive than the furniture, for just the right lamp, painting or screen may cost a mint of money.

In the living room opposite, it is the paintings that actually inspire the changeover from fern-greens to wine-reds. In the absence of any definite color predilection, taking colors from a painting is one of the easiest and surest ways to proceed. To handle a room from this starting point, it is absolutely essential to begin with a basically simple, one-color background—without patterned wallpaper or carpeting unless it is the most neutral of neutrals. The background doesn't have to be white. It might be soft yellow, pale blue or even a dark shade such as aubergine. With a dark background, as with a light one, the accessories can move from the warm red to the cool blue or green end of the spectrum. On the other hand, a whole room can be built around accessories, such as a collection of cinnabar, opaline, art glass or Creil—anything so long as it has a strong color and there is enough of it to be displayed *en masse*—a trickle of pieces is insufficient.

With a quick change of color accessories, interior designer Margaret White switched her living room from one season to another. For summer, *top*, she bared the floor, slipcovered the furniture in white, chose shades of yellow and green from the painting for prints of accent pillows, tape trim on covers.

Cold-weather scheme, *below*, revolves around red tones in the painting that in winter hangs over a sofa now stripped to its basic red upholstery. The room is further enlivened by a rich and riotous print on seating pieces and pillows. Photographs by Guerrero. Courtesy Ladies Home Journal.

No-color bedroom, *right*, cloaked in two striking black-and-white prints with the palest tint of beige in the wallpaper, is highlighted by the glint of chrome, mirror and glass in interior designer Bebe Winkler's subdued and tranquil rendering of the neutral background. Photograph by Robert Riggs.

Chic and swinging version of the black-and-white look in the bedroom of couturière Simonetta Fabiano, *far right*, was achieved through her skilled introduction of shiny materials such as plastic, steel and glass, a bed cover that constitutes the sole strong pattern in the room. Photograph by Pinto/Massey.

While it is inconceivable that color will ever go out of style, the last two decades have seen a slow but significant rise in the popularity of the non-colors—the naturals, neutrals and achromatics. These fall within the neutralized range of browns and beiges, greys, black and white. Naturals, the first to find wide acceptance, are colors taken from nature or natural materials— wood and stone, earth and sand, tanned animal hides and fur. Naturals have an innate warmth and reality that is easy to like, easy to live with. From the forties on they have been an increasingly important part of architecture and interior decoration. To appreciate the "negative" qualities of black, white and grey in combination requires a receptive and progressive decorating taste. Black has, of course, been used for centuries, deliberately and decoratively for its somber shock effect. Montezuma's Hall of Grief is an early example. Black and white in tandem is as old as the first marble floors. Black and white today is different. Through the medium of new reflective materials, arresting patterns, the "dead" no-colors come to life. Shiny vinyls and foils, high-gloss plastics, metals, glass and mirror bring the needed sparkle and gaiety to the black-and-white interior.

As the four rooms on the opposite page prove, the fact that the palette is limited is no drawback. Properly handled, it can generate a great deal of visual excitement and variety. There are many advantages to black and white. It is a restful background, a good foil for people. It presents an opportunity to play pattern against pattern in a way that would never work with color. Finally, because of the great range of tones and textures possible in neutrals, it lends itself to the subtlest and most sophisticated of effects.

With a palette of neutrals, interior designers David Hicks and Mark Hampton invested a small living room, *right*, with the controlled definition of an etching. Grey-flannel walls are offset by masses of white, patterned rug and upholstery, see-through tables, metal screen. Photograph by John T. Hill.

By mingling five major and minor patterns in a sun-room, *far right*, Louis Bromante, N.S.I.D., produced an op effect that gives black and white the visual punch of color. Wicker furniture sprayed black, black vinyl floor balance the proliferation of strong pattern. Photograph by Grigsby. Courtesy Amtico.

Naturals, while part of the large family of neutrals, play it warm rather than cool. Wood tones and textures are an integral part of the natural look, and the metals are more likely to have the golden hue of brass than the silver glint of steel and chrome. The rooms below illustrate two distinct versions of this color scheme. One, based on wood, brick, and leather, has a timeless

Natural tones ranging from the soft warm brown of saddle leather and the pinkish-brown of old brick to the smoky brown of stained wood beams combine to give a traditional country look to this living room by Barbara D'Arcy, A.I.D., of Bloomingdale's. The departure that marks it as being of our century is the introduction of bold pattern in a zebra rug, black-and-white wallpaper.

provincial quality. The other, more reminiscent of the sun-bleached landscape of California and the Southwest, relies on natural colors, rather than materials, to get its decorative message across. While wood enters into this scheme, it is a minor element. The tonal range is more extensive, embracing the yellow shades of upholstery and brass, the rust-reds of carpet and accents.

Sandy-yellow desert tones carried throughout a living room designed by Vern Kastning of Directional constitute one of the most popular decorating trends of the sixties—the warm neutrals. Teamed with wood, the glitter of brass and a rug that tends to the tawny end of the red family, the effect is more elegant and urban than its opposite number. Photograph by Tom Leonard.

The new palette of neutrals that became established as one of the major decorating trends of the late sixties differed from the earlier, nature-oriented range in being infinitely more varied and versatile. Incorporating everything from the lightest to the darkest values and a wealth of subtle, in-between tints and shades and capitalizing on the light-struck qualities of shiny-surfaced fabrics, papers and metals, the scope of the palette made possible unusual color schemes like the one opposite, where a harmony of neutrals shades gradually from beige and sand to dark mushroom and coal black. A melange of luxurious textures and shimmering accessories supplies the overtones that were once the province of beautiful woods and objects.

The constant popularity of the family of neutrals is easy to comprehend. For the majority of people, especially those too timid, conservative or inexperienced to experiment with and carry off clashing color and pattern combinations, the neutrals represent a middle ground between the over-familiar color schemes of the past and the avant-garde ones of the future. Neutrals are one of the simplest color groups to use in combination; and now, with the enlarged palette, a neutral room can appear just as stimulating and different as one heady with color.

In certain respects, the neutrals might be said to have brought to a close a decorating era when color and color schemes assumed a dominance they had never before achieved. The forties, fifties and sixties proved the power of color on the mass market. Now the seventies promise a change of emphasis in which decoration may simultaneously gravitate to the extremes—at one end the no-color room with projection and lighting taking over the decorative function and, at the other, color used in a supergraphic way to create an all-enveloping environment. As we move into an age where form and material will take on greater prestige and the solid and lasting possibly give way to the ephemeral in furnishings, it is possible only to hazard a guess at what the color trends of the next decade will be. That color, in one form or another, will remain a motivating force is beyond question. People respond, and will always respond, to the stimulus of color—human beings could probably not exist in a blanched moon-world. But as past centuries have shown, color trends are governed as much by current attitudes and innovations as by personal response. The eye quickly learns to accept and respond to certain color combinations. The only prediction that can be made is that with color in decoration, always expect the unexpected.

With a subtle and sophisticated gamut of neutrals from creamy beige to glossy black, high-lighted by the glitter of steel and mercury glass, interior designer J. Neil Stevens, N.S.I.D., gave a small living room a look of light and luxury. Photographed by Ernest Silva at Celanese House.

COLOR AT WORK

Color communicates, color attracts, color is power—these are the conclusions of the top designers and spokesmen for the home furnishings industry who keep their eye and their finger on the vagaries and pulse of consumer taste and acceptance. Boris Kroll, president of Boris Kroll Fabrics Inc. and first chairman of the Color Committee for Home Furnishings, sees this as a result of the influence of youth, with its total disregard for the old rigid rules of color combinations and color matching. Today it is the innovators, the creators who are communicating through color, not the decorating diehards. Their tools are those of the moment—new paints and plastics, synthetics and fibers. In keeping with the fast-moving, restless pace of the design world and the American population, color is now employed to a much greater degree for quick, short-term effects. It is distributed differently, in broad, forceful swaths rather than as an overall background. With industry well aware that color power spells a shot in the arm to sales, it is possible to get any effect you want, at any price. Paints come in a fantastic range of colors. Fabrics made of synthetic fibers can take an unlimited range of dyes. The choice of coloring in carpeting and flooring is unparalleled. There is no longer any reason—or any excuse—for retreating to the old "safe" colors of twenty or thirty years ago. Once you have encountered color used as it should be, with audacity and adroitness, it becomes impossible to settle for the same old conventions. Problems become challenges, and their solutions often offer spectacular contributions to the decorating scene. In our look-alike, space-starved apartments and houses, decoration is left almost entirely to the imagination—and, most of all, to color. The uses of color are manifold and magic. It creates illusion, reshapes architecture, minimizes faults and maximizes assets. The power of color to divert and direct—and occasionally to deceive—the eye is fully explored in this chapter, an object lesson in how color works on walls, floors, at windows, or in furniture and fabrics.

Family-room-kitchen develops a vital new personality through distribution of color on painted surfaces. Interior designer Duarte Pinto-Coehlo used the shock tactic of picking out strategic areas in red against slate-blue walls, white ceiling and floors. Photograph by Robert Riggs.

Stenciled design with the see-through look of a wrought-iron balcony, *far left*, was the visual device used by Ellen Lehman McCluskey, F.A.I.D., to set off a kitchen dining area without crowding the space. Red cloth, seat pads pick up the tones of the painting. Photograph by Guerrero.

A trompe l'oeil mural handpainted on the flat surface of closet doors, *left*, was the decorative disguise chosen by Mallory-Tillis, A.I.D., to add a three-dimensional look to a plain background. (A similar, less costly effect could be achieved with wallpaper.) Photograph by Tom Leonard.

The power of paint, cannily employed, can transform plain surfaces rather than merely cloak them in color. Anyone who can conjure up in the mind's eye something beyond the flat wall can capture almost any effect in paint. There is a great precedent for this. During the eighteenth century, an unembellished surface was almost anathema to the eye and the spirit. We may be less extravagant, but we are by no means less imaginative. We tend to concentrate our painted imagery in areas where the make-believe counts most. A wall of closets may masquerade behind fake napery drapery. Moldings applied in paint can look so realistic you would have to touch the wall to be sure they weren't there. Architectural details, lacking in most of today's homes simply because the craftsmanship is nonexistent, can be trumped up, trompe l'oeil fashion.

There is much to recommend the arts and artifices of color. With the exception of great historic monuments to past architecture and design, there are few venerable rooms that cannot benefit from a brightening of paint in the colors of today. Many people who buy houses worthy of restoration in the original vein prefer to cling to a palette that reflects the past. Others, more adventurous and experimental, seek new values in the classic dimensions of old rooms. There is, after all, no reason to restrict our thinking with all the visual inspiration of yesterday and today before us. Perhaps the most important contribution of this stage in the current history of color is freedom—freedom from the controlled, the contrived, the constricting viewpoints of our mothers' and grandmothers' days. We are in the midst of a *nouvelle vague* of painting rooms with an eye to both embellishment and eye-deceiving effects.

Mock moldings in stark white that delineate wall and ceiling areas of yellow and brick red were the painted deceptions with which designer Max Clendinning put his contemporary stamp on a classically proportioned room in his Georgian house, *far left*. Photograph by Michael Boys.

Painted mural in sunstruck colors was the happy inspiration with which Milan Bayan, A.I.D., brought frivolity to the walls of a garden room, *left*. To ground the colors, he reiterated the yellow, orange and pink in darker values in upholstery. Photograph by George Szanick.

Fine frame for an entrance, *right*, was created by interior designer Betty Sherrill of McMillen Inc., with half-round moldings turned and painted to resemble bamboo. Door with moldings applied in fret pattern repeats the detail. Photograph by Grigsby. Courtesy House & Garden.

Glazed wall in ripe apricot updates hall and stairwell of a traditional house, *far right*. Interior designer Jack Steinberg of The Unicorn chose the hard finish because it requires little maintenance, can be touched up if it becomes worn at the lower level. Photograph by Guerrero.

The best contemporary decorating springs from an open mind. Now that we decorate more for the moment than for the future, we expect from our materials not so much long life as the ability to produce instant effects. Because it is proven that color in paint is the quickest and easiest way to focus the eye on what you want it to see, without a large and unnecessary outlay of time and money, paints are invading areas of decorating once confined to processes requiring many days or months of painstaking labor. The equivalent of lacquer can now spread a brilliant finish over walls, ceiling, floors and furniture, with the time required to apply and dry reduced to a minimum. Any color needed to produce a desired result can be found in the precise formulas of the manufacturer's palette. There is nothing to prevent your painting an entrance door or a stairway or a piece of furniture in a strong color that will call it to the attention, yet not everyone takes the time to figure this out. Such applications of color can make the most ordinary house seem exciting and interesting. Surprises abound in houses where paint has been put to work. Consider the difference between a blank-faced, neutral-colored entrance door and one glowing in apricot or lemon yellow. Take floors—is there any reason to leave them plain wood-color when they can blossom in rich red or deep green? Color, by adding a new visual dimension, can overcome such architectural liabilities as the "problem" corner, door, beam and window—even exposed piping. It all depends how they are looked at—as an awkward element in the background or as forms in their own right, to be accentuated and viewed in a different light. The trend now is to accept, even to embrace, architectural banalities or misfits and to glorify them with color.

Forest green, in the French Canadian genre of painted floors, becomes a foil for the soft, honey-toned pine of an eighteenth-century carved armoire in the living room of an old Montreal house, *right*. The deep color serves to accentuate the wood tone. Photograph by Guerrero.

Terracotta paint makes ordinary doors the stand-out features of a once-plain entrance hall, *far right*, designed by Frank J. Lincoln Jr., A.I.D. Moldings painted black (and painted in where they did not exist) link the color scheme to the living room. Photograph by Paulus-Lesser.

Red rivets attention on a window corner, *far left*, that would otherwise be slated for decorative oblivion. Instead, Mallory-Tillis, A.I.D., turned it into an attractive seating nook by capitalizing on the painted Venetian blinds. Photograph by Hans Van Nes. Courtesy Venetian Blind Institute.

Honey-gold felt backed with Velcro makes a flexible backdrop for a collection of hair ornaments in a dressing area designed by Elaine Lustig Cohen, *left*. Tiny Velcro strips hold the lightweight combs, enable them to be changed around at will. Photograph by Louis Reens.

Color triumphs over the drab and the undistinguished. No room is so cramped, so nondescript or so uninviting that it cannot be saved by a strategic infusion of color at just the right point. Unexpected, bold strokes of color can bring "nothing" areas of a room into prominence, turning the hitherto unnoticed into the come-hither. The most minor elements in a room scheme—the landlord's Venetian blinds, found furniture from a thrift shop or the Salvation Army, an old straw or sisal rug—can be salvaged by a quick lick of paint. Color can point up a wall behind a bed or in a dressing area that would otherwise, in its natural state of neutrality, be passed over. Half the success of decorating with color is seeing the elements and areas of a room from a different, more precise vantage point. To size them up, pretend you are a camera. Hold your hands beside your eyes to limit your field of vision, or squint through a circle of thumb and forefinger as photographers do, and focus on one object, one wall or one corner, visualizing how it would look in a bright new guise. This is the *raison d'etre* of the painted accent piece, the single colorful table, chest or chair that stands out like a jewel in a room setting. By directing the eye toward one specific thing, you also distract it from any architectural drawback better ignored, a simple tactic often overlooked when decorating problem-rooms. Colors should never be strewn around wholesale—they cancel each other out. It is more practical and to the point to concentrate color where it can do the most good, have the most impact. Always consider where you want attention to be focused—toward an adjoining room, on a seating area, a storage wall or collection or on a piece of furniture with a shape you want to show—then call on color to pull it off.

Like an abstract painting, a chest of tiny drawers, each one painted a vivid color, becomes the focal point of a small dining area, *far left*. Huddle of spice jars, Mexican painting complete the wall composition, neatly framed by the sweep of the arch. Photograph by Harold Davis.

A bold stroke of cranberry red in a plastic paint that miraculously simulates the sleek texture of leather sets off work island in a kitchen designed by John Woolf and Robert Koch, *left*. Formica cabinets on cooking wall repeat the color in a shinier material. Photograph by Max Eckert.

A quartet of identical tub chairs upholstered in brilliant colors and grouped in front of a window wall accent a neutral living room designed by Joseph Braswell, A.I.D., *right*. Dressmaker detailing of the silky covers adds interest to the back of the solid chairs. Photograph by Robert Riggs.

Bold planes of color—pink, orange, violet-blue, turquoise—stripe seating pieces in a bone-white living room designed by Hans Kreiks, A.I.D., *far right*. The range of colors can be changed at will merely by recovering the sofa cushions and the seat pads. Photograph by Louis Reens.

Today, as never before, furniture is taking over the burden of color and design in rooms. As modern moves in, replacing the old linear, up-against-the-wall furniture with sculptured shapes in clingy stretch fabrics, tight as a second skin, the standard rules of furniture arrangement no longer apply. With walls now intended to be looked at or through, all those arbitrary boundaries of rooms and furniture groupings have ceased to exist.

The first breakaway came in the fifties with that architect's innovation, the conversation pit or seating pool, a radical approach to the age-old question of where to put the sofa and chairs. Now it is no longer necessary to step down in order to sit down in the comfortable environment of a square or circle of seating set off from the rest of the room. The new system of pooling color in a freewheeling seating arrangement has taken over, and there is more than comfort to recommend it. First, rules about covering upholstered furniture to match walls and carpet (thus retiring them to the background) are no longer valid. Second, against a bland white or neutral background the seating pieces now carry the weight of the color scheme, and, with prime color and, perhaps, pattern interest concentrated in them, all that is needed to change the look of a room is a quick switching around of furniture. The same pieces can also have more than one coat of color—in slipcovers or stretch upholstery—to slip into. Sofas and chairs must, of course, be shapely enough to look good out in the open, but nowadays even traditional furniture is so tuned-in to the trends in scale and grace of style that it can just as well be pulled into a center-of-the-room arrangement as lined up in disciplined symmetry.

Free-form furniture clad in tight red stretch fabric makes an inviting conversation group in a family room designed by Arthur Elrod Associates, *right*. The absence of detail in these chairs calls for really conspicuous color to draw attention to their shape. Photograph by Leland Lee.

Concentrating color and pattern in an out-in-the-open seating island, a pair of eight-foot sofas and a marquise covered in a floral print and an overscaled plaid are grouped around a two-tone shag rug in a living room designed by Bebe Winkler, *far right*. Photograph by Robert Riggs.

Parquet floor stained a striking red contrasts with the stripes of a zebra-skin rug in an unusual black, white and red bedroom by David Barrett, A.I.D. The unaccustomed floor color has the effect of pulling together all the elements in the room. Toile slipcover, striped seat pads, ticking wall continue the color theme. Photograph by Grigsby. Courtesy House & Garden.

Glazed ceramic tile floor in the deepest of azure blues, inlaid to resemble fish scales, sets the aqueous tone for the upper, river-gazing level of a living room designed by Harold Schwartz. Walls upholstered in the same fabric as the curtains echo the blue of the floor in a softer, neutralized shade, without competing with the view beyond the windows. Photograph by Guerrero.

Rugs, from accent to area to wall-to-wall, put color to work at ground level. Nowadays, when it is as feasible and fashionable to have pattern on the floor as on the wall, rugs represent a quick way to change or keynote the decoration of a room. We can expect to see in the seventies a new direction in carpeting, with more daring designs than those of the past—abstracts, graphics, fluid optical motifs, overprints. Vibrant color and pattern, once mostly confined to the custom field or to accent rugs, is taking over stock carpeting as manufacturers experiment with advanced printing techniques. The precise, geometric patterns popularized by David Hicks in his designs for Harmony Carpets are now being augmented by swirling patterns in daring color combinations conceived by couturier Emilio Pucci, a new entrant in the sphere of custom carpets, heralding a day when rugs will be as giddy and gaudy as clothes. It is all part of the color and pattern explosion that has brought into being so many design innovations. When the carpet industry, traditionally conservative and slow to change, gets with it, the revolution might be said to have arrived.

Accent rugs, small enough to be put down and taken up at whim, still represent one of the most flexible and inexpensive of all decorative elements. An accent rug can punctuate a conversation group, pave a corridor between rooms, be shown off beneath a glass-topped coffee table. Wherever and whatever it may be—plain, textured, printed, patterned, layered in colors, woven— the accent rug is designed to stand on its own. Patterned area rugs and carpeting, larger and more dominant, need to be handled differently and with a measure of discretion.

Nondirectional print of Roman shade continues over the ceiling in soft fabric waves in an unusual treatment by T. Miles Gray Associates, *right*. By drawing the eye upward it suggests height, gives the impression of a skylight. Photograph by Demarest. Courtesy Celanese Corp.

Traditional teaming of lambrequin, tie-back draperies and window shade, *far right*, was updated by interior designer Robert Crewe with one printed fabric used throughout rather than the usual combination of solid color shade and contrasting print. Photograph by Richard Davis.

There have always been two schools of thought about the treatment of windows. One would leave them as bare, visible and unmuffled as possible, allowing their architectural bones to stand out and the view beyond (which had better be good) to show through. The other holds that since windows, like walls, are an integral part of the background, they should be treated as such and linked to the room scheme through the use of color and often pattern in fabric. Certainly where the window is less than perfect—over- or undersized, badly placed or awkwardly conceived —there is much to be said for the second method. The strategic deployment of color can turn a problem window into an asset simply by making it look better than it is. Curtains are not always the best solution. To control light, create effects and "build" architectural interest where none exists, window shades and shutters have proved to be a more flexible and versatile medium. Today, there is also the tendency to treat a stock window as if it were a backdrop, blocking it out with bold color and design or hanging over it a series of window shades that can be pulled down, one at a time, to give a quick impression of pattern. With lamination, it is perfectly possible to fuse any fabric or vinyl to a shade, even to the slats of a Venetian blind.

There is much to be said for putting color at the window. In a rather stark, neutral modern room it can introduce warmth and brightness. In a traditional room, the right fabric and treatment can bring all the elements of the scheme into harmony. There can be no excuse for not being as daring with windows as with any other part of the room. They are just another of the components susceptible to change that make today's decoration more spirited than that of the past.

Narrow, fabric-sheathed slats of Venetian blinds filter pinpoints of light to create a pointillistic effect in a bedroom designed by Jack Lenor Larsen, A.I.D., *right*. Blinds and matching screens supply the main color. Photograph by Hans Van Nes. Courtesy the Venetian Blind Institute.

Frames covered with striped fabric matched to the café curtains help to reshape and unify a wall of odd-sized windows in a family room designed by Bebe Winkler, *far right*. The clean-cut frames and the regular geometric patterns go well with simple furniture. Photograph by Grigsby.

The punch of down-to-earth pattern is exploited in a living room by Joseph Braswell, A.I.D., where the black-and-white floor, designed like a parquet abstraction, pulls together a conglomerate of furniture, accessories and materials. Tangerine leather chairs and Siamese pink stool act as sharp color accents. Photograph by Grigsby.

More neutral groundwork on a grand scale, the timeless hound's-tooth motif, bridges the design gap between a Récamier chaise and contemporary furniture in a room by Emily Malino, A.I.D. The understated background permits the shapes of chair and chaise to stand out in silhouette. Photograph by Tom Leonard. Courtesy Cabin Crafts.

Every age, sometimes every decade, poses a different problem in decoration. Our age is undoubtedly the era of architectural nonentity, of rooms so utterly devoid of detail, so squeezed and limited by the rising cost of space and the proliferation of mass building that the quality of the indoor environment has become almost totally dependent on the saving graces of decoration. In contemporary apartments with their confining and badly designed floor plans, there has to be a totally new approach if we are to break out of the visual and esthetic constriction of the shell provided by the builder. Rooms must turn in on themselves and rely on color, pattern, shape and lighting to create a soothing or stimulating envelope for living. The more deficient the architecture, the more imaginative the solutions must be, for where nothing exists, it is not only desirable but also imperative to experiment. Take, for example, the room opposite, without a view or any distinguishing details, a plain four-square box. Only the boldest, most conspicuous visual device could give such a room identity and character. The designer's answer was to scale everything toward the floor rather than the walls, by covering the entire area from wall to wall with a giant fretwork pattern in tufted wool carpeting that turns it into a chiaroscuro of dark blue and off-white. The bed, which would normally have been a large and distracting element, is unobtrusively blended into the background by means of a tailored coverlet stitched with tapes in a motif that matches the carpet. A featureless room now pulsates with the exciting impact of strong, geometric patterns—the floor, the vertical, built-in shelving behind the bed, the lines of the chimney breast. Even the furniture has a forthright angularity, slightly softened in the contours, that carries through the theme of square and rectangular shapes. The secondary interest in the room is a play of accessories, books and Oriental scrolls on the bedhead wall that draws the eye up and away from the floor to this major focal point.

The new status of the patterned floor in contemporary decoration is shown in this unconventional treatment where the deliberately maximized scale of the carpet motif is the key to the whole room scheme. A geometric design like this is almost mandatory for large expanses of floor in rooms where the furnishings are very contemporary or markedly eclectic. The ageless, classic geometric forms cause no disparity between periods, and their very symmetry has the effect of drawing together furniture of different design persuasions in a serene and harmonious totality.

Color is kept under control to let pattern predominate in a bedroom designed by Joan Lerrick. The giant carpet motif is deliberately duplicated with tape in a scaled-down version on the bedspread to phase out the shape of the bed. Photograph by Grigsby. Courtesy Magee Carpet Co.

While color alone can work wonders in decoration, it is infinitely more effective in coalition with its natural ally, pattern. Color and pattern in combination have the ability to create moods —quiet patterns in neutral tones promote serenity, busy patterns in brilliant hues generate excitement. Together they camouflage architectural anomalies—jogs, beams, sloping ceilings—or make cramped rooms seem spacious and barnlike rooms cosily intimate. It has long been accepted that the easiest and most direct way to handle a multicolor scheme is to pick a printed fabric or paper that combines all the colors, then single out two or three for seating pieces and accents.

Today, while all of this still holds true, a straightforward mix of color and one pattern is no longer considered enough. Whereas it was once thought quite adventurous to combine two patterns in a room—usually a floral and a geometric such as a stripe or a plaid—now that the pattern-piled-on-pattern movement has taken over, one room may flaunt as many as three, four or even five distinct patterns. Combining patterns entails much more than putting two and two together. It requires infinitely more care and consideration than the combination of colors alone. There must be a delicate balance of scale, color and motif in order to arrive at a juxtaposition that intrigues but does not jar the eye. The more pattern, the less color is almost mandatory. With merely one color plus white or a neutral, the pattern level may be stepped up considerably to include, perhaps, a floral, a hexagon, a stripe and a supersize check. The black-and-white sun room on page 27, for instance, encompasses no fewer than five patterns distributed over walls, ceiling, upholstery and throw pillows, but the very neutrality of the color scheme cancels out their complexity. Brilliant colors, on the other hand, should be put together in a single pattern mix— stripes and polka dots, flowers and lattice, caning and basketweave. Two or more patterns need a measure of compatibility—a common, shared background either in color or design influence. In the dining room opposite, three forceful patterns in a varying scale from large to small combine smoothly because they are all drawn from nature or natural motifs and their colors come from the neutral palette. A positive approach to the partnership of patterns can help pull together a room like this where the furniture is of mixed origins ranging from eighteenth century to the most linear and unadorned contemporary.

A trio of timeless patterns cast in the neutral color range combines readily in a dining room designed by Bebe Winkler. Ceiling, walls and frames for windows are papered with a see-through fretwork motif, leopard-printed linen covers host chairs and the tile floor has the look, but not the texture, of brick. Photograph by Robert Riggs.

Capitalizing on the contemporary cult of teaming startling colors and patterns in an eye-jolting totality, Mallory-Tillis, A.I.D., generated decorative excitement in a featureless family room. With stripes and outsize polka dots taking over, furniture is kept to the straight and square line. Photograph by Tom Yee.

Equally pervasive play of traditional pattern in a sitting room designed by David Barrett, A.I.D., is more muted in color. Here the stylized symmetry of the Indienne tree-of-life printed cotton used wholesale, the needlepoint rug, lets furniture shapes and details stand out. Photograph by David Massey.

There is almost no field of home furnishings today in which pattern has not taken over in depth. The designs of carpets, fabrics and wall coverings grow steadily more audacious and the proliferation of flexible vinyls and laminates has ensured that not even a plain table or bench need lack an ornamental facade. Where fashion has led, with ever wilder and more gypsy-like extravaganzas of riotous color and pattern-on-pattern, decoration has not lagged far behind. The two fields are, in fact, overlapping more and more. Fabrics by designer Jack Lenor Larsen are as familiar in clothes as in decorating. The top names in couture have accepted the manufacturers' invitation to put their imprint on carpets, fabrics, sheets and towels. With this merging of fashion and furnishings, our sense of economic values has subtly shifted. There is no longer any necessity to live with a decorative style of which we have tired when it is as easy and acceptable to redo last season's room as to turn in last month's coat. Change comes naturally in an age when modern design is exploring to the full the potential of throwaway and inexpensive materials—paper, plastic, urethane foam. Young designers see their creations as being ephemeral and expendable; contemporary in their idiom is synonymous with temporary.

Color and pattern are undoubtedly two of the most potent tools in this kind of decorating philosophy. Both are being used today as never before; both are widely exploited in every type of material and every phase of furnishings; both lend themselves to quick-change artistry.

The room opposite presents a clear case for the new decorating flexibility. At first glance it may seem to be an immoderate kaleidoscope of color and pattern that only the young could tolerate for long. The fantastic effect of the wallpaper is doubled by the mirrored end wall, the pattern picked up in the small Parsons table, papered and coated with clear vinyl lacquer. Yet on closer examination, certain decorating sanities have been observed that make the explosion of pattern both possible and sensible. There is a lavishment of black and white in the furniture to act as a buffer, and strong geometric forms calm the exuberance of the floral motif. The major area of color and pattern is the papered wall, and that is easily dispensed with. Replace the paper with a sober wall-color—a dark or neutral shade or a soft pastel—and the visual shock would vanish. With its studied structure of shiny vinyl and plastic surfaces and shattering pattern, this is definitely a room of the moment, embodying the fashions of today. Yet only minor changes are needed to transform it into the room of tomorrow.

A psychedelic mix of vivid color and flamboyant pattern in a fractured floral wallpaper is tempered by the introduction of two black-and-white geometrics—pindot vinyl on chairs and sofa, supersize chevron on laminated table top. Photograph by Grigsby. Courtesy Lord & Taylor.

Designers and Color

Designers are visionaries. They have to be. It is their intuition, their imagination, their special antennae that sense the directions and trends of the future and translate them into furniture, fabrics, interiors. They are aware of the latest technological advances, alive to the possibilities of new mediums of expression. In their hands, plastic becomes an art form, color an emotional release, an interior the cocoon for a new life-style. Designers are the pioneers who lead us to accept unfamiliar materials, pattern and color combinations we would once have shunned. Through their continuing contributions to the fields of color and design, they have influenced our lives and our outlook in many significant ways.

SEYMOUR AVIGDOR, young original who creates atmospheres with shapes, forms and colors, carried the print-on-print explosion to its peak with his mixtures of many graphic patterns.

WILLIAM BALDWIN, noted for his timeless decorating style based on brilliant flower prints in coordinated fabrics and wall-papers, especially in his designs for Woodson.

MILO BAUGHMAN, innovative furniture designer who introduced bright color to large upholstered pieces, thus earning them a place in the center of the room, has been influential in bringing the latest developments in furniture to the young, budget-priced market.

YALE BURGE introduced and developed the widespread use of antique painted finishes, and brilliant stains for plywood paneling.

DOROTHY DRAPER, late great lady of decorating, popularized the feminine, garden-like partnership of green-and-white stripes with overscaled cabbage roses in red or pink.

ALEXANDER GIRARD, through his designs for interiors and contemporary textiles and objects for Herman Miller, brought the bold, primitive color palette of Latin America to home furnishings.

MELANIE KAHANE is credited with the perennially popular fifties color team of pink and orange and the updating of the traditional color scheme of black-and-white floor and walls with one color accent—a glowing splash of pumpkin.

BORIS KROLL, a leader in the color coordination of solid and patterned fabrics, has extended his influence to all fields of the industry, as first chairman of the Color Committee for Home Furnishings and a director of the Color Association of the United States which sets color standards and issues yearly predictions as a guide for manufacturers and merchandisers.

JACK LENOR LARSEN, known for the originality of his designs and color combinations in fabrics, was one of the first designers to give mass-produced textiles a handmade look.

ESTELLE AND ERWIN LAVERNE, innovators of modern abstract design for fabrics and wallpapers, notably marbleized papers in brilliant colors, were also the first American designers to produce sculptured, see-through furniture in plastic.

DOROTHY LIEBES, pioneer in and outstanding contributor to textile design on both the handwoven and machine-made levels, originated in the fifties the partnership of blue and green, still one of the most popular and enduring of all modern color-combinations. She also reinstated the medieval tapestry process of interweaving metallic threads for highlights, using instead a man-made fiber, Lurex.

WILLIAM PAHLMANN gave once-somber leather upholstery unusual, brilliant colors and combinations.

TOMMI PARZINGER brought about the recognition of wood colors, in a wide range from blond to ebony and gave beautiful, glowing lacquer finishes to some of his furniture.

EMILIO PUCCI translated the vivid, psychedelic colors and patterns of his famous fashion prints into fabrics, sheets, towels and rugs for the home-furnishings field.

ELSA SCHIAPARELLI, best known for shocking pink, a brilliant blue-red named for the label of her perfume, was the first haute-couture designer to enter the home-furnishings field with a collection of printed fabrics and wallpapers in high-fashion colors.

NEAL SMALL, designer in Lucite and plexiglass, brought new dimension and vibrancy to see-through furniture by the introduction of color to the material.

MICHAEL TAYLOR reinstated the ageless blue-and-white color scheme in a modern context, combined rough and crude textures with sleek, smooth surfaces in his own version of the all-white room, or the white room with a strong color accent, such as marigold or red and black.

EDWARD WORMLEY brought back in the fifties the soft jewel-like colors associated with the Art-Nouveau era, in modern fabrics, tiles, enamelware and accessories.

THE COLOR ENVIRONMENT

The end of the sixties saw decoration moving into high gear, drawing on devices used by artists and designers to evoke visual and emotional stimuli—clashing colors and patterns, surfaces that reflected and fragmented light and color, supergraphic and lighting effects that appeared to reshape the background. While most of this was chiefly practiced in the more aware and avant-garde sections of the country, the underlying philosophy was demonstrably more in tune with the dynamics of the space age and the moon shots than the "old guard" decorating styles that had survived virtually unchanged for centuries. The new direction of interior decoration, stressing the changeable and illusory, was undoubtedly the outcome of many tradition-breaking factors that had radically affected American life-styles and attitudes within the last decade. Spearheaded by the young, interpreted first in fashion and art and then in design, these factors foreshadowed a reappraisal of the role of decorating in the seventies. With a population explosion and a dearth of living space, especially in the major cities, techniques capable of expanding and altering interiors visually became vitally important. Space, once regarded as finite, was now recognized as existing as much in the mind and the eye as in actuality. While this was essentially a return to the ancient concept of trompe l'oeil, the means of producing illusion had been vastly augmented by twentieth-century technology. The new "switched-on" decoration aimed at creating a total environment for living in which furniture was minimal or stripped to its bare function as part of an overall look. This was a point of view geared to those willing to experiment, discard, move with the times. It represented an acceptance of the break-away culture of the younger generation, a disregard for the status of possessions. The room opposite capsules many of the aspects of this kind of decoration. Basically neutral, it is "decorated" with the ephemeral and inexpensive—a glossy painted wall, a foil-papered storage wall, color and pattern in accessories.

Transformation of a plain room covered from floor to conversation pit with beige tile and carpeting was accomplished with little more than color and pattern by designer Joan Lerrick. The supersized "poster" is actually a collage of metallic papers applied to storage cabinets, with paper cut-outs identifying the contents. Photograph by Grigsby. Courtesy Magee Carpet Co.

With a great swath of rainbow-like color painted on canvas sections by Honorio Morales and stretched over walls and ceiling, interior designer Jean-Pierre Borg created a room within a room. Neon-tubing light sculpture in a plexiglass table reiterates the sense of moving color. Photograph by Pinto/Massey.

Walls, flat and featureless, have always stirred the decorator in man, presenting an overpowering incitement to adorn or transform them. Not even the cave dwellers were untouched by this basic urge, as the wall paintings of Altamira and Lascaux show. The early Egyptians, Greeks and Romans, cultured and affluent, were the first consciously to enrich and enhance the walls, floors and ceilings of their sparsely furnished houses with color. While the Egyptians, ruled by symbolism, mostly painted their walls with flat colors and strong tones, the Greeks and Romans practiced the finer art of realistic and trompe l'oeil decoration, with friezes and frescoes in relief depicting everything from battles to wreaths of flowers. Theirs was an age when decoration was kept pure and simple, within the bounds of classic taste, a restraint to which the great eighteenth-century designers returned after the discoveries of Pompeii and Herculaneum.

Today, we are experiencing a revival of the painted background close to the original concept, but interpreted in contemporary terms to solve contemporary problems. After years during which walls were mostly painted in flat, solid colors, with paintings and accessories supplying the pattern, they are now being painted in ways that actually help to reshape the architecture visually, much as the Romans used street scenes to open up their windowless rooms. One example of the new type of painted background is shown on page 34, in the Georgian interior restyled by owner-designer Max Clendinning. Two other ways to redefine architecture with paint can be seen opposite. In the upper picture, one end of a long, narrow room in an old house was set off by mounting on walls and ceiling free-form bands of color painted on canvas. The curves destroy the cramped regularity of the architecture by creating a different visual pattern that lashes the eye with the impact of abstract art—which, in fact, it is. In the room below, undulating stripes of black and blue painted along the wall of a narrow area produce an oceanlike effect of limitless space. These modern methods of fooling the eye, while based on the classic art, have one great advantage—being strictly temporary, they may be removed or painted over at any time.

A painted wave of black and blue undulating along a white wall and reflected into infinity by a mirrored wall at right angles abolished the boxed-in look of a small living room, another example of the use of color and pattern to counteract or break out of architectural confines. Photograph by Pinto/Massey.

While art, in any century, has always been an accepted part of interior design, it took on a new stature and significance in the sixties, the age of the art collector who preferred the rambunctious-ness of op, pop, hard-edge and light paintings and kinetic art to the tranquillity of the Old Masters or the Impressionists. The proud possessors of works by contemporary artists who painted on a heroic scale found themselves literally hemmed in by their forty-foot, wall-to-wall canvases. As art grew ever more monumental, powerful and intrusive, the old standards of decorating "around art" had to be abandoned and another set of guidelines worked out. By virtue of its size, form and color, art became the primary force in a room, furnishings the secondary. With art taking over all the available wall space, furniture was pushed into the center of the room. For a time it seemed that the cliché of the sixties would be the white-walled, art-filled interior with a few seating pieces and end tables in natural or somber tones huddled meekly and apologetically around an area rug. The problem of harboring both people and paintings in a single room without having it seem as stark as a gallery brought forth two main schools of thought. One held eclecticism, a mingling of art and antiques, to be the answer, on the grounds that good design of any period was capable of holding its own against any contenders. The other opted for the total contemporary approach, stressing the sculptural quality of modern furniture with clean, fluid lines and an absence of detail in sleek steel and leather, glass and plastic. Gradually, in-terior designers, influenced by the display techniques of museums and galleries, began to intro-duce color in the background—primaries or deep, dark hues that served to play up the colors of the paintings.

In the rooms opposite, where the art is not overscaled but capable of being absorbed into the overall design, white is the background because white is the best medium for showing off and silhouetting the shapes and patterns of the paintings and collection. Both are balanced arrange-ments, handled in different ways, in which the art is the focal point—in one, a group of three paintings, in the other, a pair of paintings flanked by niches.

Art-oriented living room in an apartment designed by Paul Lester Wiener and Ala Damaz was blocked out with big areas of background color. Spotlights call attention to graphics massed on gold panels, sculpture and three-dimensional compositions framed by walls and partition painted in red and blue. All photographs by Louis Reens.

Modern apartments, with their flat, characterless architecture, are fair game for experiments with color, and it is here perhaps that the most successful collaborations of art and decoration are carried out. In the apartment on these pages, a succession of large rooms with acres of wall space was skillfully related by the use of panels of red, blue, yellow and brown, with the color in one area repeated by the upholstery or rug in another. The art collection—the most powerful element in the decoration—was thus brought into focus by the color of the panel on which, or against which, it was superimposed. Apart from the bedspread in the master bedroom, there is a marked absence of pattern. Floors and furniture are covered with solid color in the same hues seen on the walls, while table tops and built-ins are of colorless or unobtrusive materials.

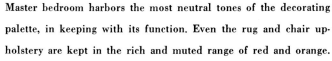

Master bedroom harbors the most neutral tones of the decorating palette, in keeping with its function. Even the rug and chair upholstery are kept in the rich and muted range of red and orange.

Study-guest-room reintroduces the red of the dining area as a backing for a storage and display wall, the leather upholstery of the desk chair. Gold and butterscotch tones echo living room, bedroom.

With huge abstract canvases firmly established on the walls of a modern room, it was but a step to the interior that was in itself an art form, with walls, ceiling, floors and furniture contributing to the total picture. Unlike Europeans, from whom the major trends of decoration had flowed in the past, Americans have always been oriented, through billboards, advertising, neon signs and commercial packaging to simple, emblematic forms expressed in brilliant colors on a large scale. The pop art movement of the sixties was a recognition and glorification of many of the aspects of mass culture, presented in an exaggerated and seemingly straightforward, but underlying satirical way. There was a humor in pop art that put people at their ease and made it possible for them to take Andy Warhol's Campbell's Soup can, translated into glassware or a wastebasket, into their homes. It was all part of a pervasive shift in values nurtured by art, movies, television and the incredible feats of the space age, in which the fantasy world of science fiction and comic strips was made fact. As designer Neal Small remarked in an interview with Home Furnishings Daily, "There has been a change in the way people perceive themselves and their environment. If we can land on the moon, why shouldn't people have light shows in the living room, or supergraphics?"

To William Woody, an art instructor at Yale University, Times Square is "The most impressive large work of art produced in the twentieth century," and his apartment, shown opposite, is as charged with visual stimuli as that American mecca. The pattern of the American flag, a design motif he favors for its pattern and color, is painted on the living room ceiling in stripes of slightly different shades of red, with silver Christmas decoration stars stuck on a panel of shiny blue. The flag design appears again as a curtain in the bedroom. On one wall of the living room he took the familiar Coca-Cola bottle display sign and turned it into a construction that spells out "O = O," lighting and framing it like a painting. On another wall, images on a light screen fluctuate and shift with the volume of hi-fi rock music. Furniture of the throwaway type picked up in second-hand shops is treated as part of the overall design by being painted or covered to blend in.

Pulsating with color, pattern and the flickering images created on a light screen by rock music, William Woody's self-designed living room might be considered the apotheosis of pop, the eye-opening movement of the sixties which first revealed the underlying significance and stimulus of commercial art forms.

Equally dramatic, the bedroom boasts a billboard background—pieces of posters assembled in a random design with bands of colored tape in between. A whirlpool of fluorescent paint swirls on the ceiling over the bed. Even the unsightly radiator is painted into the total design. Photographs by John T. Hill.

The real advances in decoration today are being brought about by the innovators, the people who think differently—designers, architects and artists who have the ability, imagination and opportunity to try something new and the wit to discard it if it doesn't work. One such innovator is Paul Rudolph, who though an architect himself does not go along with avant-garde twentieth-century architects who would dismiss decoration entirely. He believes that people have always wanted and needed to decorate, that it is inherent in man, and that it would be ridiculous and wrong to cut ourselves off from it. He changes his own apartment all the time and says, "I make experiments and sometimes I make great mistakes, but it doesn't matter. Nowadays there is a feeling that we are all moving very rapidly and therefore the gypsy aspect, the caravan aspect, is more prevalent. One out of every three or four Americans moves every year, so we are apt to think in terms of doing one thing for now, something else later. You can make a mistake and it's not forever. Anyway, I'm anti everything being the same, either in architecture or inside it. I want it to be much more human and individual."

One of his experiments was within the cramped confines of his apartment-house kitchen, opposite, which he calls, "A little Renaissance room. It's actually a kitchen enveloped by a billboard, but the idea of expanding and changing space through color and pattern is nevertheless a Renaissance notion that goes way back in time. There's nothing new about this. The pop artists have shown very clearly that the familiar takes on unfamiliar aspects when used in a different way. The kitchen is covered with panels of a Gulf billboard that originally was about twelve by twenty-four feet, a standard shape, and I just rearranged the panels. I'm of the opinion that billboards may yet emerge as the great twentieth-century art form, not necessarily used in interiors, though as you can see they do have fantastic possibilities there. We are so used to billboards and neon lighting and all those things that we tend to pooh-pooh them and think they are awful when, in fact, there is a humaneness and life to them—it's just that we don't know how to use them very well." Like other design innovators, Mr. Rudolph believes that two of the most potent sources of decoration today are graphics and lighting, both temporary, changeable, inexpensive means of transforming the indoor environment. His contention, which few would challenge, is that change depends on imagination and the power to see things in a new way, and that it is those who can think—and think differently—who lead the way, in this or any century.

Panels of a billboard, reshuffled in a giant graphic design, cover walls, ceiling and floor of Paul Rudolph's apartment kitchen, expanding the narrow, galley-like space through color and form and changing a nondescript area into a complete environmental envelope. Photograph by John T. Hill. Courtesy Time.

The breakaway of modern furniture design from traditional styling in the late sixties was a major factor in establishing a new kind of interior decoration in tune with the requirements and rationale of the coming decade. The furniture that made headlines at the Cologne International Furniture Fair early in 1970 was of a different breed. Through the use of injection molding and other speed-up manufacturing processes and such malleable materials as urethane foam, polystyrene, fiber glass and plexiglass, furniture was released from the rigid line to flow smoothly in curves, contours and sculptural shapes. With woods ever more costly, cabinetwork a vanishing art, detail inevitably had to give way to furniture that was unadorned, relying for its effect on its own space-enveloping, body-contoured beauty of form. As the outlines of furniture assumed prime importance and a high degree of visibility, color became an important asset to everything from tables to seating pieces. In some cases color was built into the basic material, in others applied in the form of stretch upholstery and vinyls or fabrics that covered upholstered-to-the-floor pieces, disguising their inner construction and giving warmth to their spare, clean lines. By virtue of its light weight and scale, flexibility and versatility, modern furniture permitted more options than ever before—a choice of uses, the possibility of groupings and regroupings within the framework of one room. Modular furniture, the kind shown in two of the rooms opposite, can be lined up against a wall, brought into the center of the room, separated into sections or massed together. With a switch of color in stretch upholstery or cushions, it can turn on a completely new color scheme. Change is an essential part of the furniture philosophy of the seventies.

During the latter part of the sixties, a unique and timely decorating trend surfaced. Dubbed the "Wet Look," it depended for its effect on the lavish use of every kind of shiny, slick, reflective surface—from the modern foil papers, high-gloss lacquers and plastics, lustrous vinyls, stainless steel and chrome to timeless materials such as glass, mirror, mercury glass, silver leaf and the precious metals. Mirrors, which had almost gone out of favor in interior decoration, were back again in strength, but no longer were they seen in the old style, heavily framed and squarely positioned over a mantel or a console table. Mirrors had a new freedom and a new function. In the form of mirrored walls and screens, mirrored surfaces, mirrored accessories and mirrored sculptures they were used more imaginatively and daringly, to introduce light and sparkle to rooms with neutral color schemes, to produce a third dimension of depth and space and to break up reflected images of furnishings, paintings, people into an exciting kaleidoscope of color with the visual stimulus of kinetic art. Mirrors became a means of liberating cramped apartment interiors from their architectural confines. Flexible mirrored sections were applied to the walls of tiny bathrooms, a mirrored wall extended the space of a closed-in foyer, a screen of mirrors shut out the view from windows facing onto a city street, mirrored doors on a storage wall belied the flatness and blankness of the surface beneath. With no outstanding decorative character of their own, merely the ability to reflect and intensify what is already there, mirrors are equally at home in traditional or contemporary rooms, mingling easily with furniture of either persuasion. They are especially effective in places where there is little or no color.

Mirrors don't just stick to walls. More and more they are appearing in accessories and in the new three-dimensional sculptures which may be bought in sections and assembled to hang on a wall or stand in a corner.

Derived from the reflective principle of the Wet Look, but a subtler, more variable extension was the metallic background, which was to bring about a great change in the complexion and potential of plain walls. Silver wallpapers, silver foil, silver vinyl and the ultimate luxury of sheet metal, through their ability to capture and reflect the fluctuations of light, color and images, introduced a hitherto untapped source of decorative diversity within an existing framework. Designers were quick to seize on the advantages of surfaces that could bounce back color and pick up cool and warm tints from natural or artificial light, neutral backgrounds that had life and sparkle. In the room at the top on the opposite page, the walls are covered with panels of corrugated stainless steel, screwed into wood strips behind, that pick up light and color all day long, from the pale orange glow of the sun's first rays through a cool bluish cast as the light fades to the yellow-gold of incandescent lighting in the evening—an effect that can be varied by switching the color of the light bulbs. While this type of installation is costly, silver foil, although difficult to hang without getting bubbles in the surface, represents a less expensive way of bringing about the same result. Then, toward the end of 1969, the Formica Company announced the test marketing of a plastic laminate for vertical surfaces that would be finished like silver, copper and bronze, a clear indication that the metallic wall was no passing fad, but a major decorative trend that was here to stay.

In the room at the bottom of the opposite page there is a fascinating glimpse of what our future habitat might be. Lino Schenal, a young Italian artist, used one silver-foil wall in the bedroom of his free-form sculptural environment, created with polyester foam within the architecture of a seventeenth-century palazzo. Doorways, walls and ceiling molded in sprayed foam melt into a series of sculptural forms that are picked up and distorted into rippling images by the bedroom's foil wall. The enchanted cavelike ambiance presages a made-to-measure environment of the future, instant interior architecture through chemical foam compounds.

LIGHT AND COLOR

The interrelationship of color and light is something we take for granted. How could it be otherwise when light *is* color, and the colors we see would not exist without it? Yet in decoration, light has usually been regarded as subordinate, a factor that influenced but did not engineer the room scheme. Wall colors were chosen for their ability to reflect or absorb light. Colored light bulbs and dimmer systems that controlled light levels were used to alter the mood of the room and its color scheme. There were the usual rules about overall lighting and spotlighting, the intensity of light required for various parts of the room, but that was about it.

Only recently have we begun to explore and exploit the infinite possibilities and potential of light itself. The techniques first of the theater and then of the discotheques have made us aware of the strong emotional responses light can call up, of its power to create illusion, produce images, alter surroundings and combine with sound and motion in mind-blowing, hypnotic effects. These are some of the aspects of lighting that the more advanced designers are now calling on to create changeable, flexible environments within stereotyped, look-alike modern apartments and housing units. They cloak rigid architecture in softening "veils" of pure light, and vary the monotony of blank walls by projecting onto them moving patterns of light and color. Lighting is no longer just something to see by, it is something to live with, and we can choose whatever effect we wish. For serenity, there is the soothing luminosity of white light reflected from white walls, for drama and excitement the eerie other-worldliness of black light, produced by black light bulbs and ultra-violet filters. Barbara D'Arcy, who designed the "white light" room opposite and a companion "black light" room, considers lighting to be a force that cannot be overlooked in decorating, and the biggest thing today for those interested in the new developments. She and other designers stress that such lighting effects are not necessarily expensive, they can be achieved with simple, easily available equipment.

Glistening like a snow maiden's cave, this dining room designed by Barbara D'Arcy, A.I.D., of Bloomingdale's is a study in the subtleties of pure light—light reflected by a mirrored tile floor, diffused through plastic columns, bounced off contoured walls of white-painted sprayed urethane foam. Photograph by Averill Smith.

Curvilinear stretch nylon walls are washed with soft light emanating from a mushroom-shaped lamp behind the dining table in designer Jack Lenor Larsen's living room. The only other illumination comes from a spot focused on the hard-edge painting by Paul Gedeohn. Photograph by John T. Hill.

To textile designer Jack Lenor Larsen, light is the most important decorative tool we have. Most people, he feels, don't take advantage of the protean quality of light because they can't see it and so undervalue its talent for changing and redefining space and surroundings. In his own New York town house, Mr. Larsen experiments with light as an artist uses paint, creating what he describes as "an almost psychedelic background, a string of moods I can walk through or sit in or work in and be excited or calm or remote." His living room, one end of which is shown opposite, is sheathed in a sculptural shell of white knit stretch nylon pulled tautly over a framework of wooden ribs in curves as smooth and perfect as an egg. Not only does the fabric reflect and heighten the level of the illumination but, with no corners to turn dark and distracting, it gives the impression of an enveloping, buoyant halo of light. One small hooded lamp is the source for the light that washes over the walls.

On pages 84 and 85 is another of Mr. Larsen's experiments, a mock-up of the kind of apartment living room he proposes as one answer to the growing confinement and depersonalization of city shoebox architecture. A built-in system of light and color projection would make it possible to dial on an instrument panel with only six controls any color or mixture of colors and patterns, either stationary or moving slowly in cloudlike formations. While such an installation would be custom and costly now, Mr. Larsen sees no reason why it could not eventually be produced with miniaturized and transistorized power sources for less than the cost of a color television set. This would be supplemental lighting, in addition to conventional plug-in or strip lights for general illumination, designed to supply a whole battery of color changes and a personal climate of light.

For now, there is an inexpensive and easily installed type of mood lighting—the black light fixture. This increasingly popular device born of the discothèque, when teamed with screens, shades or walls coated or printed with phosphorescent paint can turn on an old-fashioned room, like the bathroom opposite, bathing it in a mysterious, other-worldly violet glow.

Mural painted on bathroom walls appears in its true colors under incandescent light, *far left.* Under ultra-violet rays of black-light fixtures in ceiling, the Day-Glo paint shines and changes color, bathroom turns blue, *left.* Designed by Donald Cameron. Photographed at Celanese House.

There are many ways of decorating with light, not the least of which involves lamps and other luminous sources, including art—light sculptures and light paintings, electrically and sound controlled. Lamps, once the least inspired and interesting elements in a room, are finally catching up with the currents of change. Now they appear in all manner of imaginative, amusing and pleasing forms and colors, in plastics and metals. A floor lamp no longer looks like a straight column with a shade on top—it may be a slim, elongated posthorn of white-painted metal, a curved stainless-steel tube or even a contoured mummy-like object swathed in white stretch jersey. Table-top lamps now take such offbeat shapes as a length of coiled vacuum hose or a mass of movable pinky-orange plexiglass loops.

In the case of the Tovibulb, an invention marketed in the early 1970's, the bulb is the lamp. A nest of multiple filaments inside a silvered or gilded sphere that resembles an over-sized Christmas tree ball lights up when the bulb is switched on, bouncing reflections off the metal-coated interior. Murray Tovi, young designer of the turned-on bulb, which is more art form than illumination, predicts that his invention will enable the room itself to be the light source, with batteries of shining metal pipes and cylinders along the walls and ceiling, ready to come to life at the flick of a switch.

One of the most popular ways to bring lighting into the decorating picture is to diffuse it through fabric or translucent plastic, either plain or colored. In one living room opposite, a neon-tube light construction vibrates inside a black plexiglass table (which reverts to ebony blankness when the current is off), while in Princess Patricia Ruspoli's studio, color was introduced by putting light bulbs inside red, yellow, blue and purple plastic cubes at various points throughout the rooms. Such strategies make it an easy matter to combine light and decoration.

To explore the possibilities of integrating lighting and environment, designer Jack Lenor Larsen and luminal artist Earl Reiback teamed talents in an experimental project that demonstrates how the aspect and ambiance of a room can be changed at will through the use of four colors —red, blue, yellow and green—dialed and mixed in varying intensities or combinations. Two kinds of light, with stained glass lenses that absorb all but the desired color and mirrored lenses that bounce back all but the desired color, produce a rainbow of effects.

Curved plastic-laminate walls of tunnel-like mock room are "painted" with many hues of light beamed through diffusers and bounced off silvered contoured surfaces in center panel that runs the length of the ceiling. *Above:* as dusk settles on the city beyond the window wall, the room is warmed by a pinkish-red glow akin to sunset. *Opposite:* a progression of colors from stimulating yellow and orange to soothing green, blue and lavender can be keyed to the mood or the time of day. Kinetic light painting by Earl Reiback relates to the cityscape at the opposite end of the room. Interior design and lighting by Jack Lenor Larsen and Earl Reiback. Photograph by Grigsby. Copyright © 1968 by The Condé-Nast Publications Inc.

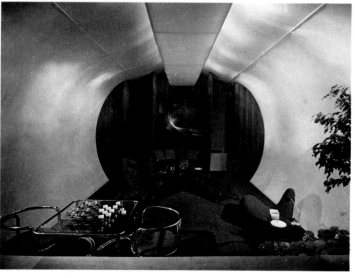

Although it is unlikely that we will see the day when decoration as we know it vanishes, to be replaced by stark, virtually unfurnished rooms where all the color, pattern and interest are supplied by computer-controlled lighting and projection, the apartment prototype opposite, brainchild of young French architect Romuald Witwicki, bears studying. Unlike Jack Lenor Larsen's lighting plan for personalizing urban apartment-dwelling, which could be duplicated now, Mr. Witwicki's "Living Envelope" is predicated on a change in social attitudes. It is geared to a future when possessions and conventional concepts of comfort matter less than the power to "turn on" one's surroundings and mind, and change will be built in through computers that move walls and partitions, furniture and lighting, program sound and color, creating an ever-new environment. The furniture is a series of mobile boxes, units and platforms that open up or come apart to provide all the essentials for eating, sleeping, sitting, storage and entertainment. These components could be transported easily from place to place, permitting a flexibility of living patterns that would fit the mobility and restlessness of a new generation.

Almost everything in the room is white—walls, ceiling, floor, window shades, platform units—with the exception of painted roller shades that pull down from a storage beam for instant backgrounds or partitions, a circle of chrome yellow that pulls apart to become a dining table and chairs, and a red-painted lighting track that supports a red hanging lamp, spotlights and mini-projectors. The color of the lighting can be changed with bulbs and filters for mood-setting, and the projectors beam images or color patterns over the blank surfaces of walls, window shades and furniture. These, and the people in the room, supply the decoration. Mr. Witwicki had a reason for this. He sees his Living Envelope as "A place designed for people—it is like an arena where they can establish relationships with each other." While this stage in living may be far off, many of the inexpensive elements of change in the room, notably the pull-down and projected backgrounds, are being used today to transform and animate the indoor environment.

Decoration of the future, as envisioned in architect Romuald Witwicki's "Living Envelope," fills an impersonal, dead-white space, blank and empty as a stage, with projected images, changing patterns of light and color that fall across the minimal furnishings—a succession of fold-down, pop-up, pull-out modular units that serve for sleeping, seating, eating. Spots on a red-painted ceiling track provide one form of lighting, projectors stream images that switch the ambiance for dining from super-cool abstractions to hot colors. Photographs by Louis Reens.

COLOR ON THE OUTSIDE

VICTORIAN HOUSE
REVAMPED WITH COLOR
TAKES ON A NEW COMPLEXION

While color on the inside of a house has been taken for granted for centuries, it is only recently in this country that color has been as confidently used on the outside. It is comparatively easy to recall the interior decoration of any given house; the colors of the room schemes are imprinted on your mind. It takes considerably more effort to remember how the exterior of the house looked, because there was no conscious attempt either to relate it to the inside or to give it a color character of its own. Traditionally, American houses have tended to the quiet or neutral tones of natural materials—grey stone, brownish-red sandstone, brick, and wood either weatherbeaten or painted sober grey, white or pastel, possibly with a stronger color creeping in for the trim. Even modern architecture puts on a colorless face through large plain expanses of glass and metal, wood and stone. When we occasionally see color used in a bold, positive way in a contemporary building, it comes as something of a shock. Perhaps we have always been a little wary of the stand-out effect of exterior color—afraid to compete with nature (a showoff who uses every shade of the rainbow with great and sure abandon) or to seem to be out of step with the neighbors. It would, of course, be a mistake to have a whole row of houses in different colors. Yet in between the garish and the drab there is a whole middle ground where color can be used adventurously, subject always to the promptings of good taste and good sense. There is no excuse for not being more imaginative with exterior color.

The houses sketched in this chapter were, in fact, observed throughout the United States. Some of their color schemes may seem at first startling and offbeat, yet each shows good color sense. The Victorian house on the previous page, for example, is one of the wooden arks left over from an age with an inordinate passion for ornamental detail. The usual response today would be to paint it into the background in an apologetic way, thereby nullifying its only asset, architectural extravagance. Instead, going on the interior design principle that an overscaled or Victorian piece is best painted to stand out rather than fade out, the shape and style are accentuated by the ochre walls, black-and-white trim and black roof. The general rule of thumb that the larger the house, the less color should be used was daringly broken and the delightful curlicues and arched windows come into focus.

The Georgian-style house at the top of this page is the kind often found in New England, where its clapboard walls are usually painted sedate grey or beige. Here they were colored violet to bring out the simple, classic lines of the architecture, with the white trim and black roof to break up the spread of color, exactly as it would in an interior color scheme based on this strong hue.

The severe geometric lines of the modern cantilevered vacation house below it would have seemed fairly nondescript if the panels that alternate with areas of glass had been neutral in tone. Instead, the brilliance of the ultramarine panels, white-and-black trim and chimney in a setting of rocky shore and soft blue water is as arresting as a poster. Now that it is possible to buy exterior paneling in colors and materials that withstand fading and salt air, this type of color is practical even by the ocean.

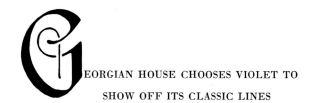

GEORGIAN HOUSE CHOOSES VIOLET TO
SHOW OFF ITS CLASSIC LINES

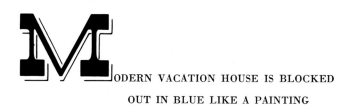

MODERN VACATION HOUSE IS BLOCKED
OUT IN BLUE LIKE A PAINTING

TUDOR-TYPE HOUSE FLAUNTS A
DIVERTING PINK FACADE

FRENCH PROVINCIAL HOUSE IS A
PAINTED SYMPHONY IN BLUE

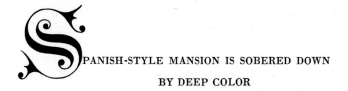

SPANISH-STYLE MANSION IS SOBERED DOWN
BY DEEP COLOR

The pseudo-Tudor house, a type of bastard architecture that had an unfortunate vogue in the 1920's, provides a good example of how really bad design can be salvaged through color. By painting the house opposite pink all over, the broken-up mixture of lines and materials was unified and the gruesome facade, which would have been infinitely depressing in the standard browns or greys, became whimsical and lighthearted, with something of the air of a Disney palazzo. Although this kind of house will never have dignity or character, it can be made acceptable and amusing by being treated tongue-in-cheek.

Houses built in the French Provincial style are extremely popular in this country, but to handle them as if they had the innate beauty of their ancestors would be a mistake. The style is, after all, a reproduction and adaptation and as such should be treated in a contemporary way, much as reproduction furniture may be. The exterior color, a light blue, was chosen from the palette of the eighteenth-century interior and transplanted to the outside. Other colors from the palette, such as the soft blue-green or pale apricot of boiserie, would have been equally good choices to show off the symmetry of the design.

Another architectural holdover from the boom days is the kind of rambling, broken-up Spanish-style mansion still to be seen in Florida and southern California, Spanish mainly by courtesy of its pink tile roof and iron balconies. For some reason this hodgepodge of roof lines, window shapes and odd excrescences is usually painted a pastel tint, which has much the same effect as seeing a dowager in a miniskirt. A good way to treat it is to make a reverse switch, forget its giddy past and darken the walls to a sober dark reddish-brown, painting the red tile roof white.

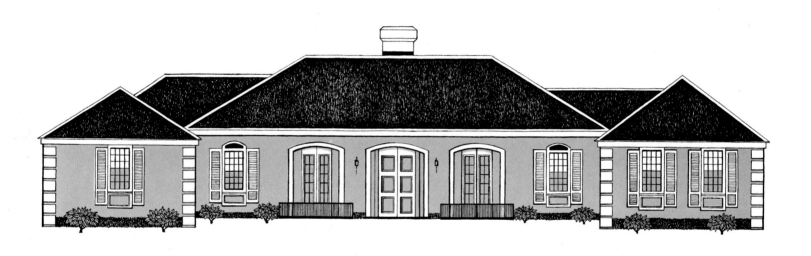

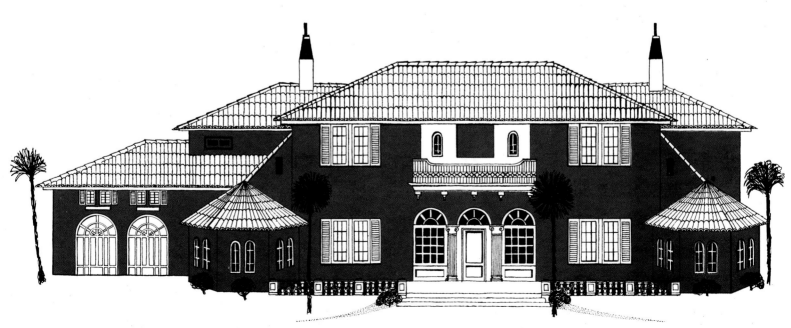

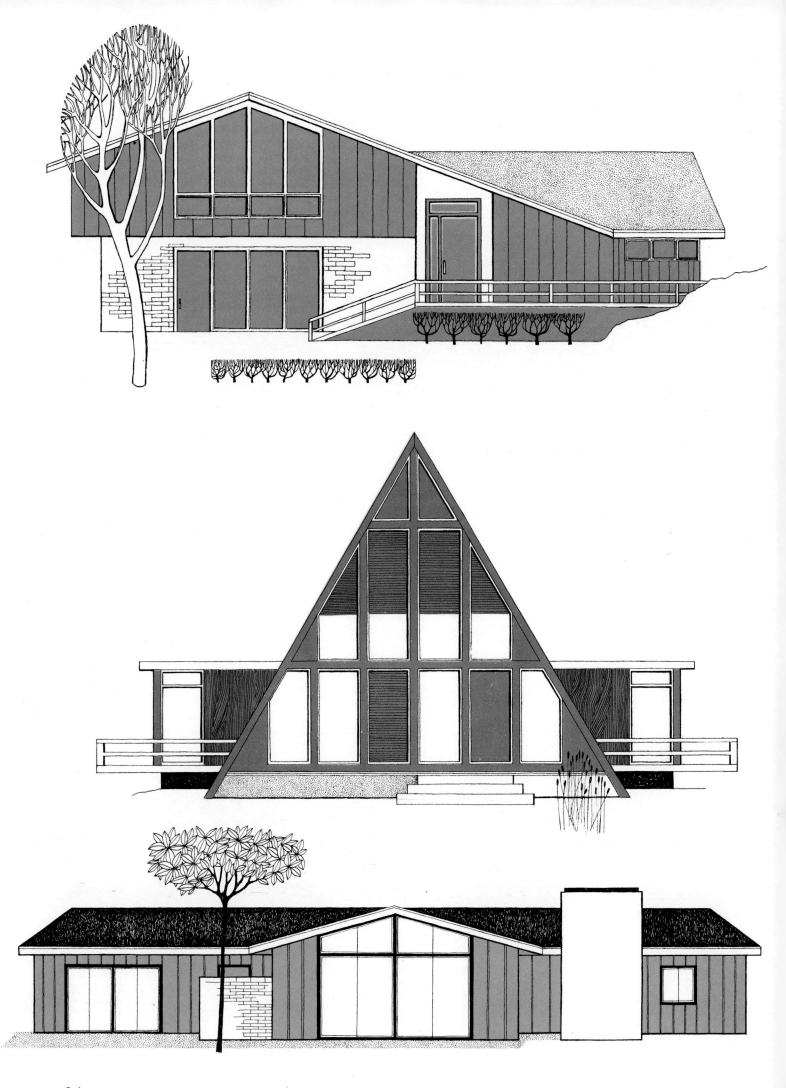

Many present-day houses, unless they fall in the expensive, custom-designed category, really have very little going for them. Plainly constructed to a cookycutter pattern, they include the builders' houses found on housing developments in every community and the pre-fabs that spring up on small lots in vacation areas. Standard in design, size and shape, they represent, after all, the kind of modest house the majority of the population lives in. If they are to have any measure of individuality or attractiveness, they must be treated with both imagination and logic. The split-level opposite is a case in point. Stained a dark fir green it becomes one with the background and the lopsided look of the two-story height is minimized.

Then take the A-frame, an inexpensive pre-fab construction that has become the middle-income vacation house because it fits so easily into any type of setting —lake, mountainside or shore. A-frames demand color to offset the big areas of glass at front and back and to accentuate the arresting geometric shape, a design plus. Stained red with white trim it stands out against a backdrop of trees, sand dunes or snow without being overinsistent. The good clean lines can take any bright color; curry yellow or bright blue would be alternatives.

The ranch house that sprawls all over the American landscape is admittedly architecturally undistinguished, but it has the minor virtues of being simple, modern and easy to deal with. Since the house is long and low, with the verticals stressed in the lines of chimney and windows, it takes only a coat of mustard paint, a black roof, white chimney and black and white trim to give it a clear-cut contemporary look that etches it against the background. Prestained exterior paneling would be a good alternative.

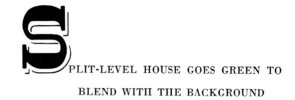

SPLIT-LEVEL HOUSE GOES GREEN TO BLEND WITH THE BACKGROUND

-FRAME HOUSE IN POSTER RED IS A STANDOUT IN ANY SETTING

RANCH-STYLE HOUSE IN MUSTARD GAINS A TOUCH OF DISTINCTION

SALTBOX STAINED AUBERGINE TAKES ON
CONTEMPORARY CHIC

REGENCY-STYLE HOUSE
IS UPDATED BY A
COAT OF YELLOW PAINT

Among the many styles of traditional houses found throughout the United States, the saltbox and the Regency are two of the most popular and prevalent. Both have the distinct advantage of being designed on clean classic lines that can stand up to a changeover from a traditional color to a more enterprising contemporary one. Treated unconventionally, the strong points of the design often become more apparent. The saltbox, a familiar fixture in New England, is usually stained a decorous grey, barn-red or dark brown, perfectly acceptable if your taste happens to run to the Early American palette. But a little flouting of tradition and a deep, rich stain like aubergine, a color by no means inappropriate to a Colonial house, can give it a sophistication in keeping with the times.

The Regency house, on the other hand, has a neo-classic symmetry that requires a light, bright color to bring out its good points. Painted a crisp, cool lemon yellow with white trim and roof, it would be particularly fetching in one of the warmer southern states, surrounded by masses of greenery and flowers. When it comes to painting houses, we too seldom take into account the partnership of color and climate, yet you have only to think of the delightful, soothing effect in tropical islands of color-washed walls faded by intense sun to the most delicate of pinks, ochres and greens, so much gentler on the eye than the blinding reflectiveness of white, to realize that color is even more important in a hot or arid climate than in a cold one. In many countries (India, Portugal and Brazil among them) exterior color, often in the form of painted decoration, has always been accepted and the execution, frequently naive and linked closely to symbolism, religion and local beliefs, is successful in striking a harmonious balance with nature.

1760

EW ORLEANS TOWN HOUSE
COLORS ITS CHARMS LIME GREEN

The living leitmotif of color that enlivens the dusty, sunbaked Indian villages and cities, the pastel tints that transform the staid Dutch Colonial architecture of Curaçao illustrate more vividly than words the power and poetry of color on the outside.

The old houses of New Orleans are one of the better examples in this country of the relationship of house to setting through color. Intrinsically elegant with their shutters and wrought-iron balconies, they become infinitely more pleasing when painted in pastels or clear bright hues. The New Orleans town house opposite, colored lime green rather than the more usual pink, fits right into its old environment yet takes on a color character that is utterly of today. Again, black and white are the accents that add a charge to the color—white trim and shutters, and black to bring out every flourish of the wrought iron-work.

In the last few years, technological advances in the manufacture of building products, paints and stains have made it possible to buy exterior colors with the same range and intensity as those used indoors. There are pre-mixed stains in beautiful colors that can be applied to any shingled or pre-stained wood finish that has never been touched by paint. The water-soluble latex or acrylic-based paints offer an even wider color choice and can be used on almost any material— wood, metal, brick, stucco, concrete, tile. Then there are all the metal sidings with acrylic-enamel finishes, aluminum shades with baked-on color, structural panels in color, even—a breakthrough in an area long dominated by drabness—roof tiles in bright colors. This, plus experimental houses being made in molded and inflatable plastic, promises that in the years ahead we will see an ever more colorful landscape.

THE LANGUAGE OF COLOR

Color speaks with two tongues, one technical, the other romantic. Certain colors are named for their historic precedents—Empire green, Williamsburg blue, Pompeian red—and can be reconstructed with a considerable degree of fidelity on the evidence of the original palette. Others, such as burgundy, orchid, apple green and sky blue, are more evocative than exact in description. This chapter endeavors to define as closely and clearly as possible the names, terms and processes relating to color in decoration, all of which have become part of the vocabulary of color.

absinthe   A cloudy green or light yellow-green reminiscent of the color of the drink absinthe. Much in evidence in the forties as a wall color, it has been revived in the sixties, under other names, and appears in all types of acoustical materials.

accent color   A color so sharp and dominant that it must be used with discretion, rather than on a lavish scale. Such colors are mostly added to a room in small doses to "accent" the overall scheme.

achromatic   Having no color. The achromatics, in decoration, are black, white, grey and the metallics.

acid dyes   Axo or naphthol dyes used on wool, silk and nylon—seldom on cotton or linen— for bright, colorfast hues.

Adam green   Considered an "antique" color because of its association with the Brothers Adam, who adopted it as a background color in eighteenth-century England. This soft greyed yellow-

Achromatic materials and patterns line a seventeenth-century colonnade of the Museum of Beja in Portugal— arches and fragments of carved stone, geometric black and white *azulejos*. Photograph by Denise Otis.

green has had a steady popularity in this country for walls, carpets and fabrics, especially as a flattering foil to the rich wood tones of walnut and mahogany in so-called "period" rooms.

advancing colors   The warm, long-wave-length colors of the spectrum—reds, oranges and yellow—which seem to bring surfaces closer to the eye. The antithesis of blues and greens, the receding colors. Also known as "warm colors."

amber   A yellow-orange named for the most familiar shade of this semiprecious stone, which is actually a fossilized resin from ancient buried fir forests. The other colors of amber are black, brown, and bright orange.

American Beauty   In decorating, a long-lived dark purplish-red akin to the color of the long-stemmed rose introduced in 1890. First a fashion color, it became a pet floor and carpet hue of the 1930's and, under other names, is still around in the home-furnishings field.

analogous colors   Closely related colors, neighbors in the color wheel—blue, blue-green, green, yellow-green, etc.

aniline dyes   Dyes derived from aniline or other coal tars; lightfast and washfast.

antique white   A greyed white with a yellow cast which has become widely accepted both as a substitute for pure white on walls and as a subtle accent for stronger colors.

antiquing   Artificial aging of wood and painted finishes by various processes. Glazes with washes of earth tones may be used to tone down the bright surface color of a painted piece, or wood given an acid bath (or bored with simulated worm holes) to make it look time-worn.

apple green   A yellow-green tint seen in green apples and Chinese porcelains of the K'ang Hsi period.

apricot   Like the fruit of the same name, a warm pinkish yellow between red and yellow-orange. This flattering, rosy shade, an eighteenth-century favorite, is currently back in fashion for home furnishings.

aquamarine   A light or medium value blue-green, similar in color to the semiprecious stone. A stayer in home furnishings because of its ability to combine well with other colors and with white.

Advancing colors—red, orange and yellow—are deployed in a rectilinear and curvilinear arrangement of painted walls, "Environment 70" furniture designed by Milo Baughman. Courtesy Thayer-Coggin Inc.

art glass A portmanteau term for the late nineteenth-century American ornamental glass blown, blown-molded or pressed into fancy forms and colors, often in imitation of agate or tortoise shell. Amberina, Favrile, Hob Nail, Peachblow and Satin Glass are some of the examples that today fetch high prices. Like other types of decorative, colorful glass, they make a pleasing accent in a room.

ashes of roses A greyed red of medium value which, in rich velvets and silks and flocked wallpapers, did much to give Victorian interiors their air of plushy opulence.

aubergine The dark rich purple of a ripe eggplant, the French *aubergine*. The color, as a glaze made from manganese, was first used on Chinese porcelains of the Ming Dynasty. The more recent fame of aubergine has been as a high-style color for walls and ceiling during the vogue for dark backgrounds.

azulejos Multicolored pottery tiles from Spain, Portugal and Mexico. Originating in the Near East, these decorative tiles were brought by the Moors to the Iberian peninsula, where they were made from the fourteenth century on. The name, derived from the Spanish *azul* (blue), was probably adopted later when the tiles were primarily colored in the traditional blue and white, a combination taken up and popularized by the Delft potteries. In Spain and Portugal, azulejos pave courtyards and fountains, face doorways, stair risers, window embrasures and appear with equal impartiality on park benches and in palaces. We mostly use them more prosaically, in bathrooms or as a floor covering for dining and garden rooms.

B

balance A figure of speech in the color world indicating that two complementary parts of the spectrum are represented in a color scheme, one balancing the other.

barn red A color that has been a familiar part of the American rural and domestic scene ever since the early settlers painted their barns with a mixture of red iron oxide (the cheapest known pigment), linseed oil and turpentine. We find it cropping up in "Early American" rooms and mass-produced painted furniture, documentary fabrics and wallpapers with a Colonial mien.

Blue and white teams with dark teak plywood paneled walls in a room designed by Inman Cook, A.I.D.

Link with tradition: wall display of antique china. Courtesy U.S. Plywood-Champion Papers Inc.

basalt   Most commonly, the name given to the Wedgwood ware which resembles in color the inky basaltic rocks of the Giant's Causeway in Northern Ireland. Basalt ware is usually self-patterned in relief, but it is occasionally decorated in the style of Greek pottery with encaustic (baked on) colors.

basic (or catatonic) dyes   Dyes noted for their brilliant colors, not always fast. They are used on cotton, wool, silk and on basic-dyeable acrylics, modacrylics and polyester fibers.

Batik in indigo and light-brown cotton. Javanese, eighteenth century. The Metropolitan Museum of Art. The Rogers Fund 1936.

batik   Originally, hand-printed cottons made in the Dutch East Indies. They were patterned in all-over geometric designs by coating part of the cloth with hot wax, then dipping it into a series of cool vegetable dyes of different colors, which were absorbed by the unwaxed portions. When the dye dried, the wax was washed off in hot water. The early batiks produced by this tedious process depended for their color on natural dyes, so they are mostly in earth tones. Now that batik is imitated by machine prints, the color possibilities are endless and the designs more brilliant.

battleship grey   Camouflage color for battleships, a drab medium-grey paint shade that virtually blended ship with water. In the 1940's it was unfelicitously adopted as a background color in decoration, a function for which it was hardly fitted.

bisque   French word for the warm tan color taken on by unglazed clay after a single firing. Biscuit is the English equivalent. White, unglazed porcelain (often used in busts and figures in the classic mold) is also known as "bisque."

black   The darkest of the neutrals and one of the most sophisticated colors in the decorating palette. Black, teamed with its opposite, white, and one strong accent color, is one of the surest and most striking of color combinations. Alone it can point up or punctuate any color scheme. A hardy perennial, emerging at least once every decade, is the black-walled room, against which other colors are played off. This decorator's shock tactic can be remarkably effective, provided it is confined to a room that is not in constant use. A milder version is the wallpaper with a black background often seen in powder rooms, entrance halls and other rooms of passage.

blanc-de-chine   A type of valuable white Chinese porcelain with a high glaze and a range of tones from a warm pink-tinged white through rich creamy and milky shades to a cool bluish white.

Blanc-de-chine porcelain unicorn kylins. K'ang Hsi period, 1662-1722. Ralph M. Chait Galleries, New York City.

bleu-de-chine   A brilliant turquoise blue which, often combined with aubergine, can be found in Chinese porcelains of the K'ang Hsi period, notably statuettes of divinities, legendary figures, dogs with dragon heads and similar fabulous animals. While the porcelains are extremely rare today, the color survives in fabrics and paint.

bleu de roi   More commonly known as "Sèvres blue," this deep blue was the first of the family of enamel-ground colors used in the Sèvres porcelain factory around 1760, and its name gracefully acknowledged royal patronage. It replaced the earlier under-glaze blue. Other factories, impressed by its superiority and smoothness, adopted the color, hence its appearance on many porcelains such as Royal Worcester. Not only china but also fabrics and wallpapers now sport Sèvres blue.

bleuet   Euphonious French word for cornflower, a brilliant reddish blue.

block printing   A form of design application dating back to the sixteenth century, and still pursued in the handcrafts field. Colored patterns or pictures are printed on paper or fabric with a succession of wooden blocks; each reproduces one part of the design in a single flat color.

blond finish   As the name suggests, this light wood tone is the product of chemical bleaching, a relatively recent treatment that works best on medium-dark open-grained woods like mahogany. Once bleached, the wood is treated with the usual furniture finishes.

blue and white   A refreshing color combination that has been in favor since the seventeenth century, especially good when teamed with dark woods such as oak. The color scheme was undoubtedly inspired by the prevalence of blue-and-white china, for up until the nineteenth century, cobalt blue was one of the few pigments that could be counted on to withstand the fierce temperatures of the potter's kiln. Some of the best known examples of blue-and-white ware are Canton, the Chinese porcelain exported to Europe from the seventeenth century on; English Worcester, Lowestoft and Caughley porcelains; Staffordshire earthenware, such as the famous willow pattern; Delftware; Meissen; and, most recently, Royal Copenhagen porcelain from Denmark.

blue persan   Another Sèvres porcelain enamel-ground blue, generally known as "turquoise." The color was thought to be Persian in origin, and so named, but in all likelihood it was inspired by seventeenth-century Chinese porcelains.

bois de rose   A rich reddish brown, from the French for rosewood.

bone white   A color reminiscent of the stark, yellowed white of sunbleached bones in the desert. Widely varied examples of bone white are the unbleached wools of Indian textiles, the subtle sand tones seen in Southwest color schemes, the bleached finishes popular in the 1930's, and off-white lacquer finishes.

bottle green   As the name implies, the deep green with a bluish cast found in the Empoli glass from Italy and Chianti and Marsala wine bottles—now also in glassware for the table.

brick red   A deep orange-red, like a newly fired brick. A color found in all types of home furnishings since the 1930's, it has endeared itself to Early American enthusiasts because it looks well with maple and pine furniture.

bright pastel   Clear, light tone of a color that has been sharpened by the addition of white.

Bristol blue   A rich, almost turquoise hue which takes its name from the widely collected opaque glass made in Bristol, England. Recently it has become a "decorator" color for walls, fabrics and wall coverings. This shade is not the original Bristol blue—that belonged to a deep cobalt-colored glass, now exceedingly rare.

burgundy   A deep purplish wine-red that was much in evidence as a fashion and furnishings color in the late thirties and early forties. Although it has recently reappeared in clothes, to date there is no sign of a revival in interiors.

burnt sienna   The yellowish or reddish-brown clay pigment that results when raw sienna is put through a "burning" process and mixed with oils. This characteristic color of Renaissance painting is used today, like burnt umber, to "grey" a wall color.

burnt umber   A dark bluish-brown earth color, also favored by early oil painters. Another pigment that can "grey" a color to which it is added.

108

café-au-lait A creamy tan, like the French coffee with milk from which the name is taken. Much favored for home furnishings in the thirties, when the rage for beige was at its height.

canary luster Pottery or porcelain with a canary-yellow ground color and a thin coating of platinum or a gold solution, which produces a silver or coppery finish.

carnival glass Also called "taffeta glass," this inexpensive, iridescent glass of the late nineteenth and early twentieth centuries, given away at carnivals and in exchange for soap coupons, was the poor man's version of Favrile. By a quirk of taste (and the fact that it has become increasingly hard to find), it is now considered a collector's item.

Celadon crackled glaze on a Chinese vase. Ming Dynasty, 1368-1644. The Metropolitan Museum of Art, gift of Wilhelm R. Valentiner, 1909.

Carrara glass A translucent glass, originally made in a milky white in imitation of the famous white statuary marble mined in Carrara, Italy. The glass, mostly used for table tops, now comes in a variety of colors.

catatonic dyes *See* basic dyes.

celadon Chinese porcelain in shades of green ranging from grey to blue, notably the greyish olive-green which once had the reputation of turning color if it came into contact with poisoned food or drink. The name may have been derived from that of the Islamic monarch Saladin, who had the porcelain brought from China.

cerise From the French for "cherry." A strong red with a blue cast.

cerulean A cool clear green-blue, the color of the sky, also known as "turquoise." As a color name, "turquoise" is slightly demodé, having been adopted at the mass level. "Cerulean" is considered more sophisticated parlance.

Chinoiserie designs on Regency black and gold lacquer bamboo cabinets. English, circa 1810. Gene Tyson Inc., New York City.

chartreuse   Named for the French liqueur of the same name, this can be either of two shades —a yellow-green or a yellow with a greenish tinge. Considered a high-fashion color for clothes and home furnishings in the twenties and forties, chartreuse, under other names, made a comeback as an accent color of the sixties.

checker, chequer   A decorative design of squares of alternate colors, copied from the checkerboard. The most familiar version is the black-and-white vinyl tile floor.

chiaroscuro   Artists' term for a play of light and shade, or black and white, in a painting or drawing. The spectacular black-and-white op art derives its effect from chiaroscuro.

china blue   The lavender-blue found in Chelsea china. A favorite wall color in the thirties when rooms were often painted this shade, with white trim, to set off Chelsea collections.

Chinese red   The brilliant orange-red of Oriental lacquer, a ranking favorite ever since the eighteenth-century vogue for Chinoiserie. In Regency times whole rooms were painted and glazed Chinese red. In the 1930's the color was revived in the craze for Chinese Modern. Today it is mainly found in painted finishes and as an accent color.

Chinoiserie   The eighteenth-century term for the various outcroppings of the European passion for things à la Chinois, first manifest in the lacquer secretaries and cabinets of the Queen Anne period, later in Louis XV furniture, Chinese Chippendale, and the ubiquitous willow pattern. In France, Pillament became famous for Chinoiserie drawings on the walls of palaces—

Checker motif carries through Mr. and Mrs. Derald Ruttenberg's dining room in superscaled slate-blue-and-white ceiling and walls, parquet squares, on chair seats and backs. Photograph by Pinto/Massey.

exotic and fanciful landscapes in the Eastern manner, as interpreted by the West. Similar decorative motifs appeared on chintzes and porcelains. The Brighton Pavilion is a famous and outstanding example of Chinoiserie in all its rich profusion.

chintz Thin cotton printed with multicolored patterns, often floral and usually glazed. Introduced in the eighteenth century when the "country look" was much in favor, chintz has maintained its decorating status, especially in England where the country-house style still flourishes. The name may come from a combination of the Sanskrit *chitra* (many-colored) and the plural of the Hindu *chint,* a later word with the same meaning.

chroma The measurement of a color's intensity. As a color in full intensity is a pure color, the chroma of a bright color is high, that of a dull one low.

chrome yellow Package expression for four tones of yellow—light, lemon, medium and orange—made from lead derivatives.

ciel bleu The pale sky blue that tinged the walls and fabrics of elegant eighteenth-century French houses. An enduring decorating color that periodically gets a new lease on life, it was reinstated in 1952 by House & Garden as "sky blue."

cinnabar Chinese lacquer work, mostly executed in the eighteenth century and highly prized today, in which the lacquer was colored a rich vermilion by the addition of cinnabar (red mercuric sulphide).

Cipriani, Giovanni A Florentine artist of the eighteenth century (1727-1785) who was responsible for the painted decorations of many great English houses and public buildings. His style strongly influenced painted furniture of the period.

citron Yellow with a brownish cast, nearer the color of the stone citrine than the fruit from which it is generally assumed to take its name.

cobalt blue A strong blue with a reddish cast, found from the seventeenth century on in the blue-on-white designs of Delft, Meissen, Wedgwood, Canton, and Bristol blue glass. Because of the toxicity of the mineral cobalt under firing, a law forbidding its use was passed in the nineteenth century. There were lackluster imitations, but the true cobalt blue was not to be seen again until the middle of the twentieth century when a way was found to produce it synthetically.

Cinnabar and blue opaline, brilliant punctuation for a neutral color scheme in a library designed by Richard Himmel, A.I.D., illustrate the role of antique accessories as color accents. Photograph by Tom Leonard.

color dictionaries   The vocabulary of color, specifically the many names adopted by colorists for identifying and describing colors. Among the most generally used are *The Dictionary of Color* by Maerz and Paul, which establishes color names with historic data for more than 7,000 colors; *A Dictionary of Color Names* published by the Inter-Society Color Council and The National Bureau of Standards, which lists and names 7,500 colors in such a way that one color vocabulary may be translated into another and color names related to the Munsell system (*see* color systems). In addition, there are the color cards issued by the Textile Color Card Association of the U.S., Inc. for the textile industry. Two sets of colors are put out each year—one according to the style and season; the other for colors in general and continuous use.

colorist   One who works with color, specifically for the home-furnishings industry.

color properties   The three distinguishing properties of color are defined as: 1) hue, or the name of the color; 2) value (or brightness), a measure of whether a color is light or dark; 3) chroma (or intensity), a measure of the brightness or dullness of a color.

color space dyeing   A process used on nylon for random or multicolor effects in which the color is dyed at predetermined spaces along the length of the yarn.

color spectrum   The rainbow range of colors from violet through indigo, blue, green, yellow and orange to red that is produced by a beam of white light as it is refracted through a prism.

color systems   Classifications and identifications of colors ranging from the simple color wheel to the more complicated Ostwald and Munsell systems described in Chapter 2. There are other practical systems used and developed by the industry, such as The Color Harmony Manual published by the Container Corporation of America, based on the Ostwald system, and the Martin Senour Nu-Hue Custom Color System, developed from eight basic paints—six chromatic, and black and white. Other paint manufacturers, notably Colorizer, Devoe, Glidden, Benjamin Moore, Pittsburgh, Pratt & Lambert have also developed color systems for interior and exterior paints.

color wheel   Conventional circular depiction of the relationship of primary, secondary and tertiary colors and their values—the tints and shades. For the decorator, a convenient guide to analogous and complementary color schemes.

Mercury glass and other silvery tones (mirror, glass, silver leaf, chrome) stamp this living room designed by Michael de Santis, *top*, as being for the seventies. Photograph by Robert Riggs.

Naturals and *neutral colors* of wood, caning, wool rugs, terracotta tile floor and pre-Columbian pottery keynote a patio room designed by Robert Brady, *bottom*. Photograph by Edmund McGrath.

color value   Semantic measure of the lightness or darkness of a color, expressed as low, medium or high value. A tint is regarded as a high-value color, a shade as a low-value color.

complementary colors   Direct opposites on the color wheel. Red, blue and yellow are the respective complements of green, orange and purple. In a complementary color scheme each is balanced by its opposite.

cool colors   Representing half the spectrum, cool colors are those with a blue or green content that suggest sky, water, ice, or foliage. Confusion is apt to creep in since red with a high blue content qualifies as a "cool" red, while green with a lot of red in it is called a "warm" green.

coral   The vibrant yellow-red of natural red coral. A firm favorite of the 1930's, first in fashion, then in home furnishings—particularly in splashy prints.

cornflower   The brilliant red-blue of the flower (*see* bleuet).

cranberry glass   English and American glassware with a clear, purple-tinged, gold-ruby color, made in the second half of the nineteenth century. Old cranberry glass, considered a collector's item, is currently being reproduced.

Creil yellow   This bright-as-a-buttercup yellow is the most common of the ground colors found in the eighteenth-century French pottery with black stencil designs made in Creil-sur-Oise. The type of decoration—subjects in a series such as months of the year or military battles—has made Creil desirable in the eyes of collectors. Other Creil ground colors are white and water-green, the latter now exceedingly rare.

crewel   A type of bold, early needlework in which coarse worsted yarns are worked on white or beige grounds. Popular in the seventeenth and eighteenth centuries, crewel is currently enjoying a revival, but in an ironic reversal, while the original designs were frequently taken from printed cottons (the Tree of Life pattern, for instance), fabrics are now printed to resemble crewel. Much modern crewel comes from India where labor is still cheap enough to make handwork profitable.

cross dyeing   A one-process dyeing for fabrics that combine several fibers. The process produces a multicolor look since some fibers absorb the color while others will not.

cyclamen   Like the flower from which it takes its name, red with a blue cast. As a color name, cyclamen was superseded by the more fashionable shocking pink, an identical shade introduced in the early 1940's, and Siamese pink, offshoot of the 1951 Broadway musical, *The King and I.*

cyanic colors   Colors with a predominance of blue, embracing the whole range from pale blue to deep purple to bluish red.

Damask printed fabric from Patterson Fabrics Inc., New York City. Photo: Miehlmann.

damask   A self-patterned and usually self-colored fabric of silk, cotton, wool or linen or, more recently, a synthetic fiber such as nylon, dacron, yourghal. Silk damask dates back to twelfth-century Damascus, hence the name. After it was introduced to Europe in the seventeenth century, Italy became a leading centre of production, and allegiance to damask as an upholstery and curtain fabric for traditional or contemporary rooms has never flagged since.

decalcomania   The prettiest of manias. A picture printed in reverse on paper is transferred to the object to be decorated (china, furniture, etc.) by first sticking the paper on and then peeling it off, leaving the design behind. This process is also known as transfer. In the eighteenth century decalcomania substituted for handpainted decoration on much Staffordshire ware, but today it has become mainly limited to, and almost synonymous with, children's painted furniture.

delft blue   Cobalt blue applied under the glaze gives Delft ware this characteristic reddish blue.

developed dyes   Dyes which are altered by the use of a chemical developer to produce a different shade or to improve light- and washfastness.

diaper   A diagonal pattern of regular repeats, usually small scale. The name comes from Ypres in France, where this pattern was woven into tapestries as early as the sixteenth century.

direct dyes   Dyes applied directly to the substrate or basic material in a neutral or alkaline bath, giving bright shades but poor washfastness.

dove grey   The tender, soft, blue-grey tint of the feathers of the dove. An agreeable color that has stayed in favor since the late eighteenth and nineteenth centuries, particularly for carpets.

dubonnet   The dark blue-red of the French aperitif. A color that was rife in the 1930's for rugs and upholstery.

E

ebonize A process by which wood is stained the glossy black of the ebony tree. It was developed in the eighteenth century, in imitation of the real wood which was then extremely popular.

ebony A deep reddish black called after the wood of the ebony tree. A favored wood of eighteenth-century English and French furniture makers, ebony was often inlaid with mother-of-pearl in the Oriental manner. It had a brief renaissance in the mid-twenties for pianos and cabinets.

ecru A beige similar to the color of unbleached linen or raw silk.

Eglomisé painting in original eighteenth-century Chinese frame. Rowland's Antiques, Buckingham, Pennsylvania.

églomisé A technique of reverse painting on glass named for and attributed to the eighteenth-century French designer Jean-Baptiste Glomy, although the customary gold or silver foil backing actually derives from the Near East. These paintings were much prized in eighteenth-century Europe and America and contributed to the flourishing trade with China—many of the pictures were painted there to the European taste and depicted Oriental figures with Western features, or vice versa.

emerald green The deep slightly yellowish green of the precious stone.

emeraude   A rich, deep, vivid green often called "Empire green" because the French Empire period was its heyday. Although "emeraude" is French for "emerald," this is not an emerald green.

Empire green   Or "emeraude." The deep yellow-green that reigned in the brilliant silks and flocked wallpapers of the French Empire. Reintroduced under this name by House & Garden, it is being taken up in the field of carpets and cottons as well as paints.

Enamel candlesticks. English, eighteenth century. Battersea. Louis Lyons, New York City.

enamel   A hard, shiny colored glaze used to decorate ceramic and metal surfaces, the result of applying powdered and moistened glass under intense heat. It may be as fine and delicate as antique Battersea enamels, or as simple and rudimentary as the contemporary enamel ware from Hong Kong. Cloisonné is enamel in which minute metal dividers, or *cloisons*, separate the different enamel colors. If the pattern is embedded in tiny pits or depressions, it is known as *champlevé*. On wood, an enamel finish is obtained by brushing or spraying on paint and then rubbing the surface with pumice stone and oil until it shines like satin. Paints with a high gloss are referred to as enamels.

faience, fayence   From Faenza, an Italian town that was a prime producer of majolica, this is the name given by the French to a type of glazed earthenware made all over Europe from the sixteenth to eighteenth centuries—Delft and Majolica are two well-known examples. In early faience from Egypt and the Near East, metallic oxides were painted on the raw glaze before it was fired, and the colors were limited to blue, yellow, orange and brown. Later faience was decorated on top of the glaze and then refired at a lower temperature, which permitted the use of brighter red and pink enamels.

Famille jaune, verte, rose early nineteenth-century Chinese covered jars. Charles Hall Inc., New York City.

famille jaune, rose, noire, verte French names given to the predominant ground colors found in the polychrome designs of the Chinese porcelains of the Ch'ing Dynasty, which dated from the middle of the seventeenth century to the beginning of the twentieth. As the first literature on Chinese porcelains was written in French, the names were adopted into general usage. Verte (green) is the earliest of the ground colors, and the more spectacular pieces have brilliantly colored enameling and refinement of design. In famille rose, much exported, the opaque pink enamel ground color is of European origin. Yellow and a lustrous black are the dominant ground colors of famille jaune and famille noire respectively. The latter, frequently overdecorated, is the least attractive of the family.

Famille noire Chinese vase from the K'ang Hsi Period 1662-1722. The Metropolitan Museum of Art, The Michael Friedsam Collection, 1931.

Flocking on wallpaper and similar grande luxe trappings bring an air of Victorian opulence to color-related rooms designed by Everett Brown, F.A.I.D. Photograph by Tom Leonard. Courtesy House & Garden.

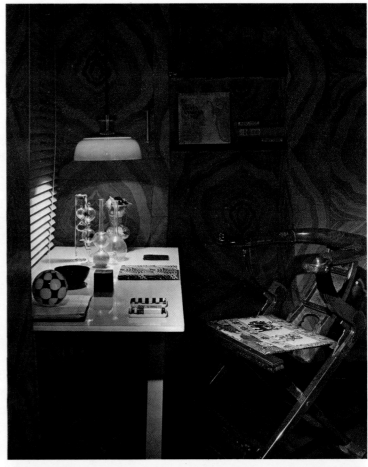

faux bois   False wood—a painted surface that imitates wood. The graining is usually exaggerated and the color does not always duplicate the real wood tones.

faux finishes   Simulations in paper, paint and plastics of real surfaces such as wood, marble, malachite, lapis lazuli, mosaic and ceramic tiles, leather and fur. *See* faux bois, faux marbre.

faux marbre   False marble—a form of fabulous fakery that apes the original material at a fraction of the cost, which gives it an edge over the real thing in decorating. Faux marbre effects are found in paint swirled in marbleized patterns, papers that simulate or exaggerate the color and grain of marble or uncannily lifelike vinyl facsimiles for floors.

Favrile glass flower vase by Louis Comfort Tiffany. The Museum of Contemporary Crafts, New York City. Photo: A. Burton Carnes.

Favrile   Late nineteenth-century iridescent case glass noted for its exotic coloring and fantastic decorative shapes, of which the best known and most coveted today is the work of Louis Comfort Tiffany. Other types of Favrile are Durand, and Aurene, made at the Steuben Glass works in Corning, N.Y.

Faux finishes on walls and floors make a decorative point through exaggeration and color. *Top left:* painted graining and knot holes on plaster walls. Photograph by Beadle. *Top right:* larger-than-lifesize marble patterns in paper. Interior design by Bernard Devaux. Photograph by Pinto/Primois. *Lower left:* Real wood cabinets with fake graining, trompe l'oeil doors. Interior design and photograph by Max Eckert. *Lower right:* Vinyl floor tile interpretation of malachite. Interior design by Burge-Donghia, A.I.D., N.S.I.D. Photo by Hans Van Nes. Courtesy Amtico.

flambé   A rich copper glaze, akin to sang de boeuf. Originated for the Chinese porcelains of the K'ang Hsi era and still popular, the glaze is characterized by streaks of grey, purple, lavender or blue in the red.

flocking   A Middle Ages stratagem to make inferior cloth resemble cut velvet, this technique involves applying a powdered material, usually wool, to the surface of fabric or paper by means of an adhesive. Flocked paper wall hangings were introduced in the seventeenth century and by the eighteenth the walls of great houses were covered with beautiful papers wholly or partially flocked. Not only silk and wool, but also such outré substances as powdered chalk, shells and metallic dust were built up in layers to give a shimmering two- or three-tone effect. Now, because the process is expensive, flocking is no longer regarded as a decorative disguise, but as decoration in its own right.

floriated   Decorated with floral motifs. A term often applied to wallpaper and fabrics with a floral design. If the surface is completely covered, the design is called millefleurs.

forest green   A deep blue-green reminiscent of trees in the depths of the forest. A favorite wall color of the 1930's.

French grey   A soft grey with a slight purplish tinge. A familiar wall and carpet color in the days before World War II.

fresco   A painting done on plaster while it is still wet and fresh (*fresco*). The term is often mistakenly applied to any type of wall and ceiling painting, technically murals. Fresco painting, a difficult and demanding technique that had to be executed swiftly and surely, was known to the early Egyptians and Romans, but it undoubtedly reached its height of glory in the works of the great Italian fresco painters—Michelangelo (the Sistine Chapel); Raphael (St. Peter's); Caracci (the Palazzo Farnese); and Giotti (the Scrovegni Chapel in Padua). Today easier methods such as tempera painting have largely replaced fresco.

fuchsia   Purple with a reddish cast, of very high saturation and medium brilliance, like the blooms of the plant from which the name is taken. In the 1950's, the Siamese-oriented musical, *The King and I,* brought fuchsia into fashion as an accent color—one of the many "hot" hues that graduated from the stage to home furnishings.

full tone   A color with full chromatic value.

124

Gallé (a) enameled glass bottle with stopper. French, late nineteenth-century. The Metropolitan Museum of Art. Gift of John C. Moore, 1940. (b) carved glass vase. French, circa 1896. The Metropolitan Museum of Art, gift of Edward C. Moore, Jr., 1926.

Gallé A type of art glass named for Emile Gallé (1846-1904) leader of the Ecole de Nancy, a flourishing center for the nineteenth-century style based on romanticized interpretations of nature known as Art Nouveau. Gallé's signed work, which embraces carved, enameled and inlaid cased glass vases and a glass he originated called *clair de lune* in which the sapphire tint changes under light, shows a complete mastery of the art of glassmaking. Original Gallé pieces, many of which were shown at the Paris Exhibition of 1878, are now much prized and priced accordingly. The work carried on after his death, although it bears his name, lacks the master's expertise and inventiveness.

garnet Plush color associated with the Victorians. A deep red named for the stone, also popular in Victorian jewelry.

gilding The golden artifice that transforms the bare face of wood, stone, metal, plaster or leather. The technique was first developed by those master craftsmen and cosmeticians the Egyptians, who invented a method of applying gold that had been beaten into thin wafers, the origin of gold leaf. The basic processes of water gilding, oil gilding and fire gilding (for metal) have remained unchanged for centuries, although most metal is now gilded by a process similar to silver plating. Vermeil is a surviving example of fire gilding. For the type of gilding most employed today for furniture, picture frames and book bindings, small, thin layers of gold leaf are applied and fixed with adhesives.

Giltwood carved Chippendale overmantel. English, circa 1760. Florian Papp Inc., New York City.

giltwood   The Midas touch that turned plain wood (pine in England and America, oak in France) to gold. The standard method, developed in the eighteenth century, is first to carve the wood, then apply a thin layer of gesso (plaster) and gild it, using the oil or water technique. The term giltwood is often mistakenly used for wood that has been covered with silver leaf over gesso and then coated with lacquer to simulate gold.

glaze   The glassy coating that gives pottery, porcelain and stoneware its smooth, shiny finish and nonporous quality. The Chinese were the first to experiment with colored glazes for ceramics, adding all kinds of substances to produce a subtle and varied range of colors and effects.

glazed walls   A painted fantasy finish. A painted wall is coated with glazing varnish in a contrasting or matching color and the varnish is then brushed or wiped with cheesecloth before it has had time to dry, producing the desired strié, stippled or mottled finish. The strié effect, which suggests the grain of wood, is often used in conjunction with moldings to give plain plaster walls the appearance of paneling.

gouache   A bilingual word that comes, via the French, from the Italian *guazzo,* to splash—*dipingere a guazzo* means "to paint in watercolors." In gouache painting, often used for murals, the water colors are mixed with gum or some other thickening agent that renders them opaque.

graining   An artful simulation of the natural grain of wood with paint, graining is often exaggerated and does not always duplicate the true wood tones. The technique, also called *faux bois* (false wood), has been practised since the time of the early Egyptians, reappearing periodically in Regency England, Colonial America and again today, as a decorating device to give plaster or cheap lumber the look of an expensive wood.

grasscloth   A handmade wall covering of loosely woven grass glued or stitched to a paper backing. Although the modern trend to texture was responsible for the popularity of grasscloth in the United States, it actually originated about two thousand years ago in China. Even in this age of mass-production, grasscloth is still dyed, woven and backed by hand (and at home) by craftsmen in Japan and South Korea, where the raw materials (reeds and hemp) are grown, and then collected and shipped by exporters.

greyed pastels   The soft pastels, muted by grey, as opposed to the bright pastels. One falls on the dark side of the color line, the other on the light.

grisaille   A type of decorative painting in gouache or oils confined in color to various tints of grey (*gris* in French) and depicting figures in relief. Grisaille was much favored in the late eighteenth century for interior wall panels and for commodes in the Adam style decorated with medallions showing classical subjects "en grisaille." Such famous Italian painters as Tiepolo and Guardi were noted for their work in this monotone medium. Artists still use the technique, although it is seldom found on furniture today.

Grisaille wallpaper panel used as a painting. Nancy Haywood Antiques, Los Angeles.

gris Trianon   An example of things being not always what they seem. This pale grey with a bluish tint seen today on the walls of the Petit Trianon bears no relation to the original color, white, but is strictly a product of time and grime.

ground color   The base or preliminary color on which other colors and designs are imposed.

half-tone   A color that can claim only half its chromatic value, halfway between black and white.

henna   This reddish-yellow brown of medium saturation and low brilliance, named for a dye extracted from the leaves of the henna plant, is one of the earliest colorings for fabrics, pottery—and human hair.

high-key colors   *See* key colors.

hue   Comprehensive term for the name of a color within the spectrum, such as red, blue, yellow, orange. A hue doesn't have to be pure to claim the family name; it can be one of many tones, from light to dark (pink is a hue of red). A tint is a hue lightened with white; a shade is a hue greyed with black.

hunting pink   This sportingly named color is not, in fact, a pink at all, but the brilliant scarlet of the coats worn by the English fox-hunting gentry. Considered an appropriate shade for game rooms and studies in the 1930's, it is now most frequently seen in upholstery fabrics that resemble woolen coating.

hyacinth   A delicate violet blue favored for paint and fabrics during the English Regency and French Empire periods. The name is derived not from the sweet-scented flower, but from the mineral corundum, a gem the ancients called hyacinth.

Imari   A heavy white Japanese porcelain decorated in blue, red and gold. Imari takes its name from the port and was originally developed for export to Europe, which explains its lack of affinity with the mainstream of Japanese design. The Imari designs were adopted and adapted by the English potteries of Worcester, Derby, Spode and Minton, for their "Japan" patterns. Antique Imari is hard to find and much more pleasing than the cruder, twentieth-century examples.

imperial yellow   A yellow as strong and clear as the yolk of an egg, often found in rich silks and velvets, but originally in Chinese porcelains of the K'ang Hsi period. The depth of color varies from light on white unglazed porcelain to a darker shade on the glazed.

indigo   A reddish blue, formerly the dye of the indigo plant, now manufactured synthetically. One of the earliest dyes, indigo appears in many of the Colonial calicos.

inlay   A decorative design made by inserting shaped pieces of ivory, marble, metal, exotic woods, glass, tortoise shell, mother-of-pearl or semiprecious stones flush with a surface. Mosaic, marquetry and intarsia are forms of inlay.

Inlay of trompe l'oeil intarsia paneling in the private study of Federigo de Montefeltro, Duke of Urbino, Ducal palace at Gubbio. The Metropolitan Museum of Art, the Rogers Fund, 1939.

ivory   The off-white color, lighter than cream, of elephant tusks and whale teeth. Ever since natural ivory was made into decorative objects, this color has been popular in decoration. The Chinese took the subtle tint of their white lacquer from ivory and today it is looked on as a harmonious ground color for fabrics and porcelains, or an alternate to chalk white for walls.

J

jade   A value of yellow-green named for the green version of the Oriental stone (it can also be white, brown, yellow and pink) and frequently found in Chinoiserie wallpapers and fabrics.

Japanning on a Pontypool coal tureen with floral decoration. **English, circa 1820. Caledonian, Winnetka, Illinois.**

japanning   The seventeenth-century vogue for lacquered furniture brought about this poor man's imitation of lacquering in which layers of varnish are applied to the surface of wood, metal or other materials, frequently papier-mâché. Most japanning is black, but colors and transparent varnishes were also used. Japanning remained in favor in England and America throughout the eighteenth and nineteenth centuries, but has since declined sharply in popularity.

jaune jonquille   Like its namesake the yellow jonquil, this eighteenth-century Sèvres porcelain ground color is a soft, fresh shade of yellow.

jet   A glossy lustrous black named for the semiprecious mineral the Victorians made into jewelry, buttons and trimmings. Black calendar paper and patent leather have the same shiny quality.

Kakiemon   A colored-enamel decoration on porcelain credited to the seventeenth-century potter Sakaida Kakiemon who worked at Arita, Japan. Kakiemon's delicate, refined designs were widely copied by European potters at the English porcelain and Meissen factories and today the word "kakiemon" describes decorations inspired by the original porcelains.

Angelica Kauffmann is credited with this painted canvas screen with classical figures. Edward Garrett, New York City.

Kauffmann, Angelica   A Swiss painter and decorative artist who worked in England, 1766 to 1781, painting portraits and classical pictures and designing painted wall and ceiling panels in the Neo-Classic style for the Adam Brothers, and porcelain plaques for Wedgwood, many of which were used to ornament cabinetwork of the period.

kelly green   A variable color that can range from a strong yellowish green to a hue slightly lighter than emerald. Since green is the traditional Irish color, it is hardly surprising that it should have been given a name so reminiscent of the Emerald Isle.

key colors   Another term describing color value. Bright colors are in "high key," dull colors in "low key." The key color can also be the predominant color in a scheme.

Kakiemon polychrome design on a Chelsea soft paste vase. English, circa 1755. The Metropolitan Museum of Art, gift of Alfred Duane Pell, 1902.

L

Lacquer Queen Anne settee in rare creme color with dark brown and gold decoration, circa 1730. Gene Tyson Inc. New York City. Photo: Albert L. Waks.

lacquer   A build-up of several layers of colored—and sometimes opaque—varnishes on wood or metal. The name comes from the basic substance, a resin lac. Originating and extensively practiced in India, China, Japan and other Far Eastern countries, lacquering is distinguished from painting by richness of color and a diamond-hard finish that will withstand years of wear.

lamp black   A jet-black pigment color culled from the smoke given off by burning oils.

lapis lazuli   Ultramarine blue. Once obtained by the costly process of grinding the stone and purifying it, this was a prized pigment first used in twelfth-century Europe. Since 1828 the color has been reproduced synthetically and is much more common. The stone has been incorporated into objets d'art, such as urns and jewel boxes, since the days of the Assyrians and Babylonians, but today anyone can have the same effect for considerably less cash by investing in accessories with a *faux lapis* finish, in paint or ceramics.

lime green   A variable color in the yellow-green range, yellower and duller than viridian, greener and darker than parrot green. Much in evidence during the 1930's in home furnishings, it still remains a popular color, especially as an accent.

lime white   A wash of lime and water, usually called whitewash, which for centuries has been slapped on the exterior and interior walls of houses.

low key colors   *See* key colors.

magenta The name given to this unusual shade of purplish red commemorates the battle of Magenta in Italy, fought around the time the dye was first made. Today magenta is found mainly in rich fabrics, as an accent color.

malachite The strong yellow-green of the semiprecious stone beloved of the Tsars. The best examples come from Russia; they are now virtually unobtainable. With the real thing hard to come by, *faux malachite* is flourishing in painted finishes on table tops and boxes and that versatile pretender, vinyl flooring.

marble One of the most protean and long-lived materials in the field of art, architecture and decoration, marble is a limestone endowed with a fantastic color range—from white and grey to green, blue, purple, red, orange, and black. Historically, it has been utilized for everything from the buildings and sculptures of antiquity to modern cigarette boxes, ash trays and similar trifles.

marbleizing A painted pretense, either literal or exaggerated, of the markings of marble. This false front can be painted directly on a surface or first painted on paper and then applied. No matter how extreme the design, marbleizing should always simulate "cut" and "fitted" marble in logical shapes. The art of *faux marbre* flourished in eighteenth-century France and Italy as a means of getting grand effects in rooms at a nominal cost.

Marbleizing (faux marbre) on top of a Régence writing table. French, circa 1730. Gene Tyson, New York City. Photo: Helga Photo Studios Inc.

mauve A delicate hue in the purple-violet range, indelibly associated in decorating with the turn-of-the-century "Mauve Generation" and now back in style because of the current interest in all manifestations of Art Nouveau. Mauve, one of the first of the aniline dyes, was discovered purely by chance in 1856 by William Henry Perkins, during an attempt to make quinine artificially.

Mazarine blue   A deep, brilliant color found in Chinese ceramics of the K'ang Hsi period. In France and England it was known as Mazarine blue, presumably because of some tenuous association with Cardinal Mazarin who lived during the reign of Louis XIV when many Chinese colors were given French names.

Meissen blue   The distinctive cobalt blue of the onion pattern (actually not an onion at all, but a fruit-and-flower pattern) and other porcelains from the Meissen factory.

mercury glass   A type of silvered glass made during the mid-nineteenth century in imitation of sterling silver. The interior of the double-blown glass was coated with silver nitrate, the exterior often etched or decorated. Decorative accessories of mercury glass—vases, bowls, candlesticks, épergnes—both old and new are popular again today, in line with the fashion for silvery metals, vinyls and fabrics.

metallic colors   The colors borrowed from metals—gold, silver, chrome, steel, pewter—which have recently begun to play a decisive decorative role in contemporary room schemes. Other aspects of this trend are plastics with metallic finishes, shiny threads incorporated into woven fabrics.

metameric color match   A method of color matching two materials that have been colored with different dyes or pigments and are identical in color under some lighting conditions but not others.

milk glass   A name shared by two types of glassware. One, of nineteenth-century American origin, is a translucent white. The other, eighteenth-century Bristol milk glass, comes in many colors, notably a soft turquoise blue similar to opaline blue, which should not be confused with the deep cobalt shade of glass known as "Bristol blue."

millefleurs, millefiori   Literally, a thousand flowers. The French millefleurs was originally descriptive of a Chinese porcelain decorated with an all-over pattern of flower heads, but now implies any such pattern. The Italian millefiori usually refers to glass paperweights in which the flower pattern is formed by bunching together slender rods of glass, slicing them across and encasing them in a glass orb.

Millefleurs Baccarat paperweight, circa 1845-50. The Metropolitan Museum of Art. The Sylmaris Collection. Gift of George Coe Graves, 1930.

Ming yellow   A rich sulfur-yellow glaze found on Chinese porcelains of the Ming period. Today porcelains in this brilliant hue, still available in reproductions, add a striking color accent to a room scheme.

monochromatic   In decorating, a term that describes a color scheme in which one color family (a single color in all its gradations) is teamed with one or more of the achromatic colors— white, grey, black, silver and gold.

mosaic   A decorative inlay technique practiced since Roman times. Small pieces of wood, stone or colored glass are set in stylized or conventional patterns or pictures as a decoration for walls, floors, furniture, bathtubs and so on.

Mosaic panel showing the Empress Theodora, copy of detail from the Church of San Vitale, Ravenna. Byzantine, 6th century. The Metropolitan Museum of Art, Fletcher Fund, 1925.

multicolor   Composed of many colors. The name can be applied to a color scheme in which three or more colors are used in one room, or to a printed fabric or wallpaper which combines several tints and shades.

nasturtium   The bright cadmium yellow of the flower, an accent color of the late 1950's.

naturals   The colors, generally but not always neutral, that are based on natural materials.

neutral colors   Such no-colors as black, white, and the metallics—gold, silver, platinum, copper, bronze, pewter and steel—qualify as neutrals, a category that also embraces tints and shades with a predominantly grey or brown cast.

neutralized colors   Colors dulled by the addition of grey or black (also known as greyed colors) or by being mixed with a small amount of their complementary colors, which destroys their purity of hue.

nile green   The yellow-green tint nicknamed "apartment-house green," a color promoted by landlords and now rarely seen.

no-color scheme   The bleached look of all white or white plus neutrals that was the decorating innovation of the twentieth century, especially for contemporary rooms.

obsidian   A lustrous satiny black which takes its name from the volcanic glass discovered, according to Pliny, by the Roman traveler Obsidius. During the French Empire, the Egyptian campaigns brought obsidian into the forefront of fashion as a material for household objects.

ochre   A natural brownish yellow pigment, used in lieu of black to deepen colors.

off-white   All-embracing term for the many yellowish or greyish whites—cream, oyster, beige—seen in wall colors and in room schemes where tones of white, in different fabrics and textures, are combined.

ombré   From the French word denoting a shaded or graduated effect in tones of one color, or in different colors. In fabrics, the effect is used to suggest a stripe.

one-color scheme   Also known as "monochromatic." A scheme based on various tints and shades of a single color, often with black or white as a catalyst.

op colors   The strong primary and secondary colors of the spectrum, such as red, blue, orange and purple, juxtaposed in clashing combinations that have the visual effect of seeming to move and vibrate. Black and white is another pulsating op combination. Introduced in art, then quickly adopted for fabrics, vinyl plastics and table accessories, op colors have progressed from accent to background for those strong enough to take the visual assault.

Opaline blue in nineteenth-century French pieces: oil lamp (electrified), sugar box (for cigarettes), saucer (ash tray). David Weiss, New York City.

opaline colors   The iridescent, pearly colors borrowed from the opal and translated into the translucent French opaline glass. Opaline, especially the expensive nineteenth-century pieces, is much collected and the most admired colors are a blue bordering on turquoise, a vibrant yellow-pink, and a green close to apple. Opaline is now reproduced from the old French molds, and in Venetian glass.

orchid   A medium-to-light lavender fashionable in the late 1920's, when the flower symbolized chic and affluence. Now considered demodé, except in combination with other colors, particularly in Thai silks.

oxblood   *See* sang de boeuf.

Painted furniture. Modern buffet. Courtesy Yale R. Burge Inc., New York City.

painted furniture   Delightfully decorative furniture which dates back to the early Egyptians and reached a height of artifice in the exquisitely ornamented pieces of Versailles. Italian craftsmen were especially skilled at painted finishes and their copies of the elegant court furniture of France, often with painted simulations of inlays and marble, gave rise to a whole genre loosely termed "Italian Provincial." In this country, the naively decorated dower chests and chairs of the Pennsylvania Dutch show the German and Swiss influences imported by the settlers. Although contemporary painted furniture is currently much in vogue and new processes have been developed for applying the paint on a mass-production basis, the best examples are still handmade, as few craftsmen today can equal the splendors and subtleties of the antiques.

papier-mâché   Expressive French term for a fanciful art long practiced in Persia and the East, which was taken up in France in the eighteenth century and had its heyday during the Victorian era in Europe and America. Papier-mâché is paper pulp mixed with glue, chalk and sometimes sand, pressed, molded into forms and baked, then japanned and decorated with views, figures, flowers and such added embellishments as mother-of-pearl inlays. All kinds of objects were turned out, from trays, screens, vases and boxes to tables, chairs and cabinets (for strength, the papier-mâché was sometimes molded over wood frames). Most of the pieces we find today are Victorian, although Kashmir is still a source of fine craftsmanship.

Glazed walls of rich red in a paneled library designed by Burge-Donghia, A.I.D., N.S.I.D., represent an updating of an eighteenth-century technique with strong, contemporary color. Photograph by Hans Van Nes.

Papier-peint wallpaper panel by Dufour, "Paris Fête." French, circa 1795, Mann & Fleming, London. Photo: A. C. Cooper, Ltd.

papier-peint   The French term for wallpaper painted or printed to suggest or simulate a painting or mural.

pastel   A technique of painting or drawing with dry pigments or colored chalk, also called crayon drawing. Pastel was an art form frequently utilized by the great masters to make studies for projected works, and the drawings are now collected in their own right.

pastels   In decorating, the soft whitened-down tints of a color.

patina   Softening effect on surface color and texture that comes with age and wear. On wood furniture the shellac, oil or varnish finish tends to darken, though still retaining its transparency, while silver and other metals take on a deeper luster.

Painted furniture spans centuries in technique, style, color. *Top left:* Venetian trompe l'oeil secretary. Interior design by Melanie Kahane, F.A.I.D. Photograph by Grigsby. *Top right:* Louis XV desk painted to tie in with bedroom color scheme. Interior design by Richard Himmel, A.I.D. Photograph by Tom Leonard. *Lower left:* Campaign chest with a coat of vinyl lacquer. Interior design by Betty Sherrill of McMillen Inc. Photographed by Ernest Silva at Celanese House. *Lower right:* Painted buffet color-linked to upholstery. Interior design by Burge-Donghia, A.I.D., N.S.I.D. Photograph by Hans Van Nes.

140

peach bloom   Chinese porcelains of the K'ang Hsi period which took the graceful shapes of such classic forms as a chrysanthemum vase and a writer's water jar. The color varies from pink to a liver shade, with brown and greenish mottlings.

peachblow   American case glass of the nineteenth century characterized by colorings varying from white to rose, greenish yellow to red, and light blue to pink, and named for the Chinese peach bloom ware it was supposed to resemble.

peacock blue   A light, bright greenish blue with the iridescence of the feathers in a peacock's tail. Imported to Venice in the rich silks from China, the color traveled to France where it was much in style in the late seventeenth and early eighteenth centuries. As an accent color it is still approved today and promises to take over in larger areas, such as carpets.

Pekin glass   A translucent glass imitative in color and design of exquisite and expensive Chinese porcelains, that might be called the opaline of the Orient. The colors range from creamy white and yellow to violet and turquoise blues, apple green and sang de boeuf. The late nineteenth century saw the first appearance in the West of Pekin glass, the 1920's its greatest vogue. Now it is a collector's item.

Pekin glass (a) eighteenth-century Ch'ien Lung carved glass vase on which later Pekin glass was based. The Metropolitan Museum of Art. Bequest of Edward C. Moore, 1891. (b) nineteenth-century Chinese carved glass vase. The Metropolitan Museum of Art. Bequest of Edward C. Moore, 1891.

period color scheme   A particular color combination characteristic of an historical period such as French Empire, Adam or Victorian. Paint and wallpaper manufacturers often take their inspiration from famous restorations like Versailles and Williamsburg, reproducing the exact colors and patterns found in the rooms and naming them after their forbears. Williamsburg blue and Adam green are examples of period colors still current today.

periwinkle blue   A variable light purple-blue, redder and deeper than lupine, found in Pekin and other art glass and today in home furnishings and table accessories, especially glassware.

Persian blue   A pale red-blue, lighter than powder blue, found in Persian rugs. Under this and other names, a moderately popular shade for fabrics and carpets.

pickled finish   The whitish patina caused by particles of white gesso that linger after paint has been stripped from wood. It is now simulated by rubbing white paint into the grain of furniture or walls, where it supposedly gives a "country look" similar to that originally caused by the flaking of whitewash.

pigment colors   The basis of all paint colors, made from natural or synthetic materials. Pigment colors include chrome yellow, cadmium, cobalt, ultramarine, viridian, raw and burnt sienna and lamp black. They run the gamut of the painter's palette.

polychrome   Many colored. Originally the word referred to a style of Greek painting that flourished in Athens during the latter part of the 6th century A.D., but it came to be applied to furniture and objects that were elaborately painted and often gilded, and to antique porcelains in two or more colors.

Pompeian red   The vibrant vermilion found in the wall paintings of the ancient city of Pompeii.

pontypool   English tole or japanned ware made from the seventeenth to nineteenth centuries, originally in Pontypool, South Wales, by Thomas Allgood and his son. The pieces, mainly small useful household objects such as tea and coffee pots, tea caddies, trays, and coal buckets were decorated with flowers, Chinese figures and scenic views in gold and colors.

powder blue   A rich blue which is given a mottled or white-speckled look by powdered pigment blown onto the oiled surface through a pipe covered with gauze. The color, noted for its ability to combine well with gilt decorations, was first used on Ming porcelains and later on those made in Europe and America.

primary colors   Red, blue and yellow. The three pure, unmixed colors from which all others are derived.

priming color   The first or prime coat of color applied to an object that is being painted. If the final coat of paint is to be a pale color, the prime coat is generally a light tint of that color, or white. If the color is to be dark, the prime coat is a deep value.

prismatic colors   The spectral colors that occur when a beam of sunlight is diffracted through a prism. *See* spectral colors.

Prussian blue   A deep greenish blue originated in 1704 by a Berlin color maker called Dies-bach from compounds of ferrous and ferric iron. This intense color has remained popular for fabrics, carpets and accessories.

psychedelic colors   Strong vibrant colors usually combined in clashing combinations to pro-duce a decorative stimulus of the senses akin to the swirling bold color effects of LSD-induced psychedelic visions. In patterns and paints, these colors often have the effect of seeming to reform or reshape backgrounds.

R

raw sienna   Reddish-brown clay pigment used for tinting. The raw material for burnt sienna.

raw umber   Earth-tone pigment with a dark greenish-brown cast used like raw sienna for its tinting qualities.

receding colors   Colors such as blue and green which by appearing to move back or "push the walls out" give an impression of space. Also called "cool colors."

roller prints   Designs printed by means of engraved metal rollers on wallpaper and fabric. Each roller prints only a single color, but the process allows many colors to be printed at high speed. The technique of roller printing, with wooden rollers, was introduced in England and France during the latter part of the eighteenth century.

rose pompadour   A soft rose-pink enamel ground color introduced in Sèvres porcelain around 1757 and flatteringly named for the factory's patroness Madame de Pompadour, who would have been irked to know that the English erroneously call this color "rose du Barry."

rouge de cuivre   French term for the coppery-red underglaze used on Chinese ceramics of the Hsuan Te period (1426-1435).

royal purple   A rich red-purple associated with rulers since the days of the Caesars—hence the phrase, "born to the purple." This exclusivity was undoubtedly due to the fact that the dye was originally made by crushing the shells of certain types of Mediterranean snail—and it took a costly 240,000 shells for a single ounce of dye. Now that the dye is made synthetically, any man can feel like a prince by decking his bathroom towel rail or living room sofa in royal purple. This color is also called "Tyrian red."

saffron   An orange-yellow named for the ancient dye and spice made from the dried stamens of the winter crocus. Saffron, as a dye, is associated with the Romans and with the colorful robes of the Buddhist priests of India and Tibet. The Siamese color schemes of *The King and I* brought saffron into the fashion and home-furnishings fields.

sang de boeuf   Vividly dubbed "oxblood," this is the French name for the deep, mottled blood-red glaze, turning a rich sherry-brown in areas of coagulation, developed in China during the K'ang Hsi period. Revived in the nineteenth century and again in the 1930's, when vases of this color were turned into lamps, the color is with us again mainly in reproductions of the original vases, lamps and other accessories.

Sanguine drawings in a wall grouping designed by Ferris Megarity. Photo: Otto Maya.

sanguine   A drawing in red crayon or chalk. Sanguines done by great artists as sketches for oil paintings are now valuable as well as decorative. The name is derived from the ground-up hemotite or bloodstone (sanguine) from which the color was made.

sapphire   Like the stone from which it takes its name, a color of infinite variety, predominantly purplish blue with a touch of green, deeper than hyacinth or Mazarine blue. Favored for home furnishings since the eighteenth century, sapphire appears in everything from fabrics to Venetian glass ash trays.

satin glass   A late nineteenth-century product, this American art glass was composed of an inner layer of opaque glass with colored indentations overlaid with colored glass, covered by an outer layer of clear glass and exposed to acid vapor baths to produce the satin-like surface.

scale blue   The color of the fish-scale ground that surrounded painted panels depicting exotic birds and flowers on early Worcester ware. Occasionally the panels were left blank to allow the decoration to be filled in by an artist.

scarlet   A vivid yellow-red of obscure but ancient origin, a venerable standby for clothes and home furnishings. The name is variously attributed to a rich fabric from Arabia and the old French word for a cloth of fast-dyed red.

screen print   Printing technique for wallpaper and fabric developed in France during the nineteenth century in which designs are applied with individual screens, originally of silk, but now also of nylon, metallic thread or paper. A single screen is used for each color in the design, with the color brushed or squeezed through the cutout part of the screen onto the material to be printed. The original hand process, although still used in the craft field, has mostly been superceded by mechanization.

secondary colors   Orange, green and purple. The products of mixtures of equal parts of the primaries.

sepia   The yellow-brown fluid taken from the sacs of such slippery sea creatures as octopus and cuttlefish and used by artists since Roman times as a watercolor and ink.

Sèvres blue   *See* bleu de roi.

shade   The greyed or neutralized result of mixing black (or an unequal proportion of opposing colors) with a pure color to produce a darker value.

shagreen   A dyed skin with a natural texture of tiny overlapping scales or circles. Although much shagreen is dyed green, the name comes not from the color but from the French *peau de chagrin* (ass's skin), one of the sources from which it is made—others are the skins of sharks and dogfish. The unusual surface of shagreen makes it a hard-wearing and attractive covering for accessories from eighteenth-century writing sets to modern cigarette boxes.

shocking pink   Intense blue-pink identified in fashions of the thirties with the designer Elsa Schiaparelli and, under that name, an accessory and background color of the forties. Now more commonly called "Siamese pink."

Staining, an age-old artifice, transforms the natural tones of wood. *Above:* celadon stain on built-in storage wall blends it with bedroom color scheme. Interior design by Burge-Donghia, A.I.D., N.S.I.D. Photograph by Grigsby, Courtesy House & Garden. *Below:* Prestained plywood in charcoal tone with red indoor-outdoor carpeting makes a way-out kitchen color scheme. Courtesy U.S. Plywood-Champion Papers Inc.

Siamese pink Catchy, cashing-in name given by House & Garden magazine, in the wake of the trend-setting colors and costumes of Broadway's 1951 hit, *The King and I,* to the strong, vibrant blue-pink that had been known in previous incarnations as "shocking pink" and "cyclamen." A perennially popular accent color in decorating.

sienna An orange-yellow earth pigment containing iron oxide, named for Siena, Italy, where it was first found, and an important component of the artist's palette. Now produced synthetically, this color has recently cropped up in fabrics, wallpapers, carpets and painted finishes as part of the so-called "Mediterranean Look."

sky blue *See* ciel blue.

solution dyeing A process used to dye synthetic fibers while they are still in a liquid state, resulting in good clean colors and lightfastness.

spatter A decorative technique in which colors were spattered or splashed on a solid-color ground. Two well-known examples are the eighteenth-century English spatterware made in Bristol and Liverpool, a type of pottery in blue, brown, yellow or purple with fan- or shell-shaped medallions, in the style of the then-popular Chinese wares, and the painted spattered floors decorated with an all-over design or marked-out panels common in Colonial America.

spectral colors The rainbow colors of the spectrum that occur when white light is diffracted through a prism. The dominant spectral colors in the rainbow are violet, indigo, blue, green, yellow, orange and red.

split complementary A complementary color scheme in which three colors are used; for instance, yellow and its complement violet with the addition of purple or blue are split complementaries.

stained glass A form of decorative art dating back to the Middle Ages in which color was fused into glass in the melting pot and, later, the kiln. Devised for the adornment of great cathedrals and churches, stained glass eventually embellished houses too. The Victorian and Art Nouveau periods saw a great revival of this art form. Today, because of its cost, real stained glass is limited to small areas, such as room dividers. For large-scale use its jewel-like tones are simulated in plastic.

staining A method of coloring wood with a stain first used for furniture in seventeenth-century England. The coloring agent then was a reddish oil stain containing vegetable dye. The seventeenth century favored black and red stains, but in later centuries, following the fashion for pale wood finishes, lighter yellow colors were adopted. Today in keeping with our more brilliant decorating palette it is not uncommon to see a floor stained lime green or bright yellow.

stenciling   Decorative technique of applying a design to a surface by covering it with a stencil pattern on oiled paper and brushing paint, dye or stain through the cut-out openings. This inexpensive, easy way of adding pattern to plain walls, floors, doorways and furniture was widely practiced in Early American houses. Today we are witnessing a revival of this venerable art—this time around on such unexpected surfaces as window shades and fireplace breasts.

stipple   Originally, a way of giving a soft mat finish to walls covered with oil-based paint by pounding the wet surface with a stipple brush which obliterated previous brush marks. On freshly plastered walls, the rough-textured look of old plaster can be simulated with the same process, using a brush or piece of burlap or crumpled paper. Now the laborious process is considerably simplified by applying a special, extra-thick stipple paint.

stock dyeing   A process in which yarns are dyed before spinning or blending, producing good colorfastness and lightfastness.

sulfur   A bright greenish yellow with the hue of the chemical. A favored accent from the seventeenth century on, and now popular as a background color.

sulfur dyes   Water-insoluble dyes used mainly on cotton to produce inexpensive dark shades with fair qualities of washfastness and lightfastness.

tapa   A rough cloth fashioned in the islands of the Pacific from the bark of the mulberry or breadfruit tree and decorated with geometric patterns in earth tones. The cloth, hard to imitate, is sold mostly to tourists or kept for ceremonies, but it has been copied in fabric and wallpaper.

tempera   A water-soluble pigment paint. The addition of the white of an egg, a trick used by the great masters, makes the paint more permanent.

terra cotta   Like the clay from which it is made, the color of terra cotta ranges from pale buff to deep red. Traditionally associated with Greek and Roman sculptures and reliefs and the tin-enameled terra-cotta works of Andrea della Robbia, terra cotta is found today mainly in interiors as a floor material—in the form of tiles imported from Spain, France and Mexico.

tertiary colors   In-between colors resulting from mixing two of the three secondary colors (orange, green and purple). The proportion determines the tone. Tertiary colors are also known as intermediates.

tête de nègre   Descriptive French term (in translation, head of a negro) for a rich black-brown color with a purplish tinge introduced in the eighteenth century and frequently found in lacquer pieces, or as a wall color in a high-style decorating scheme. To obtain the best and deepest color, a coat of black is applied, allowed to dry and then covered with a coat of Vandyke brown oil color thinned with glazing liquid or varnish which lets the black show through.

tie and dye   A hand-printing process in which small areas of the fabric are tied with thread and then dipped in the dye colors, forming a design. When the thread is tightly knotted, the dye does not penetrate and leaves a ring of ground color. When tied loosely, the dye penetrates, giving the fabric a blurred look.

Tiffany glass   Or, more correctly, Favrile glass. The late nineteenth century glass made by Louis Comfort Tiffany, among others. Tiffany's work, distinguished by its fantastic designs and shimmering iridescence, was signed Favrile, or L.C.T., or with his full name. It is the most sought after, the most expensive and, with today's resurgence of interest in Art Nouveau, the most widely copied glass. The leaded glass shades and table lamps are especially prized.

tint   Light value of a color made by mixing color with white; in decorating, often called pastels.

toile de Jouy   The felicitous French name for the finely woven printed linens and cottons originated in 1760 at Jouy. The designs, mostly pictorial and often of classical scenes, are printed in one color on a white or natural ground and remain as much in the decorating foreground today as they were in the eighteenth century.

tole   Painted metalware, especially tin, turned into such decorative but useful objects as trays, teapots, coal scuttles, candlesticks, chandeliers, lamps, jardinières and boxes. The most celebrated examples of tole were made in France and England from the late seventeenth through the nineteenth centuries, and America has some charming, if naive, native pieces. The most common of the tole ground colors are black, deep red, mustard yellow and olive green. Blue, white and tortoise shell are the rarest. There is still a steady demand for tole, both the contemporary ware and reproductions of the early designs.

tonal value   The gradations of one color, from light to dark. Pink is a light value (or tint) of red; maroon is a dark value (or shade).

top dyeing   A process used to produce thread used for color blending in which fibers are combed and spun on tops and then dipped in vats, forcing the dye through the fibers.

150

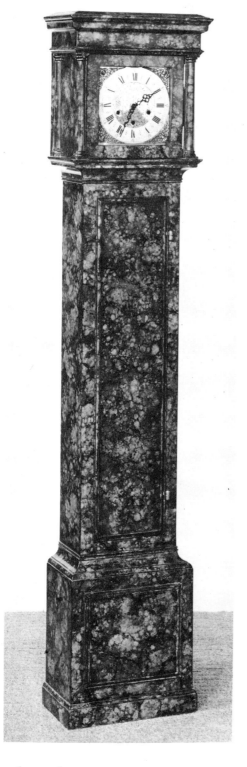

tortoise shell   The beautifully colored and marked shell of certain sea turtles, particularly the hawksbill. As an ornamental element in decoration, it reached its height in the metal and tortoise shell marquetry of André Charles Boulle, the famous cabinetmaker of the Louis XIV period. In the eighteenth century, tortoise shell —often tinted red or green—was used as a veneer on boxes, tea caddies and similar small decorative objects. Today, due to the high cost of the real thing, the rich brown tones and subtle shadings are often emulated in plastic or paint.

transfer   *See* decalomania.

Tortoise-shell painted finish on a grandmother's clock from Smith & Watson, New York City.

Tole oval tray in red lacquer with gold decoration. Grace Ellis Antiques, Los Angeles.

triadic color scheme   A color scheme which uses three colors equidistant on the color wheel (i.e., yellow, blue and red; orange, green and purple) or values of these colors that belong to the same family. The triadic color scheme is used in two ways to give a multicolored effect—in muted tones for the traditional look, in vibrant colors for a modern or psychedelic look.

Trompe l'oeil window shade by David Barrett, A.I.D. Courtesy Window Shade Manufacturers Association. Photo: Dennis Purse.

trompe l'oeil Decorative deception in paint or paper designed to "fool the eye," either for practical purposes or as a charming conceit. In Pompeii, the walls of rooms were painted with realistic vistas of the world outside. Later centuries saw painted trompe l'oeil versions of architectural details, costly marble and boiserie, or furniture ornamented with make-believe but lifelike depictions of three-dimensional objects. Now, when painted versions can cost as much as, or more than, the real thing, wallpapers have pretty well taken over the trompe l'oeil field.

turkey red A moderate red made from iron oxide widely used in American Colonial days and now in documentary prints on fabrics and wallpapers. The name was probably derived from the Turkomen rugs of Central Asia, noted for their rich reds.

turquoise A brilliant greenish blue that takes its name from the mineral of the same color. Probably introduced to Europe in the eighteenth century through the silks of the East, it has been a steadfastly popular accent color ever since. It is also known as "cerulean," the name given to the color by House & Garden in 1951.

Tyrian red Another name for royal purple, the ancient dye color extracted from snail shells found on the shores of Tyre. Its current use is primarily as an accent color.

U

ultramarine A brilliant blue with a reddish cast, sometimes called "French blue." Originally the pigment was made by pulverizing lapis lazuli. This was a favorite color of the great masters.

umber A color that takes its name from the brown earth used by artists as a pigment, either in the raw state or calcined (burnt) to give it a reddish cast. In decorating, raw umber is added to "grey" a white to an antique white for walls, or to "antique" a painted finish on furniture.

underglaze   Decoration or color applied to china under, rather than over, the glaze.

underglaze color   The pigment color with which pottery is decorated before glazing.

union dyeing   A one-process dyeing of a combination of fibers, such as silk and dacron, to produce the same color in each one.

V

vat dyed   Dyed after weaving.

vat dyes   Water-insoluble dyes made from indigo, anthraquinone and carbazole which can be used on all types of fibers. The dyes most resistant to washing and sunlight.

vegetable dyes   Dyes from natural substances—animal and mineral as well as vegetable. They are usually expensive and have a limited color range.

Venetian red   An orange-red pigment color, originally a natural product of the earth but now made synthetically from iron oxide and calcium sulfate. As an undercolor, it gives a rich and rosy glow to gilt furniture and gilded mirrors.

verdigris   A greenish-blue poisonous pigment produced by the action of acetic acid on copper. Dating from Roman days, this was one of the earliest artificial pigments. Throughout the centuries it has been widely used for outdoor metal furniture and garden ornaments, although seldom in interiors.

vermeil   Gilded silver or bronze with a warm rose tone (vermeil is French for vermilion and it is the vermeil, or rouge, mixed with gold amalgam that gives the metal its color). Vermeil or argent doré (silver gilt), which resembles gold in everything but price, is included in French inventories as far back as 1316, but its credit soared in the reign of Louis XIV when it replaced the gold plate confiscated by the crown and melted down to fill the royal coffers. Now vermeil is no longer looked on as a canny substitute for the more desirable gold but a sought-after shining asset to any table.

vermilion   A vivid red, shading from crimson to orange, that takes its name from the fiery pigment originally made from cinnabar, and beloved of artists. Under such pseudonyms as "lipstick red" or "fire-engine red" it can be found throughout the range of home furnishings.

vernis Martin   A brilliant glossy varnish finish for furniture developed during the reign of Louis XV by the Martin brothers, probably in an attempt to emulate the luster of the more durable Oriental lacquers. Today it is simulated, in its turn, by plastic finishes.

vignette   In painting, the gradual shading-off of a subject. In decorating, emphasis placed on a particular area of a room by pinpointing only that portion.

viridian   A cool, transparent yellow-green of medium saturation and brilliance. First introduced in Paris in 1838, the pigment was made by a secret process eventually published in 1850 by Guignet (the color is also known as Guignet's green). From the artist's canvas, it found its way into the decorating palette, where it has remained ever since.

warm colors   Those colors in the red and yellow half of the spectrum that suggest sunlight and flame. Also known as "advancing colors," these attention-getters have the effect of making walls seem to close in and space shrink, or of making a small object look more important.

wash   A thin mixture of one color applied over another, similar to a glaze.

Wedgwood blue   A light purplish blue that takes its name from the best-known of the Wedgwood pottery ground colors. In decorating, primarily used on the walls of period rooms.

Wet Look   One of the decorating fashions of the sixties that arose from the prevalence of and vogue for surfaces that were shiny and slick—foil, patent leather, mirror, glass, chrome, steel, high-gloss lacquer and plastics. The Wet Look, which could be found in furniture, fabrics and accessories, was achieved not so much through color as through materials.

white   The lightest of the neutrals and the one most universally relied upon to accent, punctuate or relieve a color scheme. Stark white walls have long been regarded as the best foil for contemporary art or bold, bright colors. Lately the tend has veered to the softer values of white—the off-whites—which are frequently combined, in varying textures and materials, for the all-white room scheme.

white lead   The base for all but the darkest oil paints. White lead gives the paint its covering quality when mixed with linseed oil.

Williamsburg blue   The greyed green-blue uncovered during the Williamsburg restoration; a trade name used by the Martin-Senour Company and by far the most popular color in the Williamsburg paint palette for exteriors and interiors.

Wood colors with their natural gradations of tone and texture lend a primitive strength to the interior of a ski lodge faced with rough-cut wood in the raw. Design by Derek Parmenter. Photograph by Fred Lyon.

wood colors   The natural tones of furniture and veneer woods, ranging from white to the deep black of ebony. They include:

ACACIA   A veneer wood similar to locust. The colors vary from yellowish brown to red and green.

AMARANTH   Also called "violet wood." A veneer wood with a strong purple cast.

AMBOYNA   A wood primarily used for veneers and inlays. It has highly mottled and curled burls and takes a high polish. The color ranges from pale orange to a light brown.

ASH   The wood from a family of trees used for furniture—many Windsor chairs are of ash which has a color range from a light honey tone to a warm brown. The beautifully figured burls are prized for matched veneering.

ASPEN   A variety of white poplar valued for its yellow-white satiny veneers.

AVODIRE   A highly decorative veneer wood with a satin-smooth luster and a color range from milky white to pale yellow.

BAMBOO   Although it is often painted, in its natural state the wood of the bamboo is a pale honey beige. Popular for generations as a furniture wood, and for decorative objects.

BASSWOOD   A lightweight, white, soft wood employed primarily as a corewood for plywood or as the base for inexpensive painted furniture.

BIRCH   A light-colored wood, both hard and soft, probably the most popular structural wood, next to gumwood. It can be stained and finished to imitate more expensive cabinet woods such as walnut and mahogany.

BOXWOOD   A light-yellow wood with a firm, close grain. Mainly used for inlays, carved or turned articles.

BURL OR BURR   A diseased or abnormal growth on a tree, sliced into cross sections for veneering. The cross sections show beautiful mottled or figured patterns in a variety of colors, depending on the tree.

BUTTERNUT   A decorative wood, similar to black walnut but lighter in color.

CANE   A pale yellow-beige, this flexible rattan is mainly woven into chair seats and backs, headboards, boxes and place mats.

CARPATHIAN ELM   A light reddish-brown wood with dark veinings favored for tabletops and chair backs.

CEDAR   A red-colored wood noted for its fragrance, first used in eighteenth-century traveling chests as a protection against moths and now as a lining for closets, drawers and boxes. Bermudian furniture is often made of carved and turned cedar.

CHERRY   A warm red-brown wood of the American colonists, it also appeared in European country furniture, and extensively in Biedermeier and other nineteenth-century styles. Much reproduction Provincial furniture is made of cherry.

CHESTNUT   A grey-brown wood with a coarse, open grain, especially suitable for wall paneling or the table tops of country furniture.

CIRCASSIAN WALNUT   A highly figured wood from the Black Sea area which has irregular dark strippings on a light-yellow ground.

EBONY   A hard, deep-black, fine-grained wood which takes a high polish. Popular for furniture since Roman times.

ELM   A tough, light-brown wood, much like oak. The Romans made furniture from it; we chiefly make frames. The American, English and Carpathian elms are the most prized for veneers.

HAREWOOD   A grey-green wood from sycamore and maple trees which is stained or dyed and used for veneers. A popular furniture wood in eighteenth-century England.

HICKORY   A hard, tough wood that resembles oak in color and texture. As it is hard to work, its use is mainly confined to rustic furniture.

KINGWOOD   A veneer or inlay wood with a rich, deep, black-violet color streaked with gold and dark brown. Favored in the Queen Anne and Georgian periods.

LAUREL   A hard, deep-brown wood with a pronounced wavy grain. The East Indian variety is the best known.

MAGNOLIA   A light wood the color of straw with straight grain and uniform texture used for veneers and the exposed parts of furniture.

MAHOGANY   A wood that changes its color according to the taste of the times. Its unrivaled position as a fine furniture wood began in the eighteenth century in France, Italy, Spain and England, where it is enduringly associated with Chippendale. During the French Empire, fashion dictated that mahogany be a deep, lustrous, highly polished red. In the American Federal period it became an over-varnished deep black-red. Today we prefer either the more natural soft red-brown tone of the Georgian era or, for contemporary furniture, a bleached greyed brown.

MAPLE   One of America's most popular furniture woods, probably because of the prevalence of the tree and its ability to be carved and turned with ease and polished to a high finish. It has a great variety of figure and texture—curly, bird's-eye, wavy blister and quilted—and a color range from white to yellow-brown. Although most commercial producers of maple furniture for the mass market have stained it an unfortunate red-brown, supposedly the color of Early American antiques, the early Colonial furniture was not this shade at all, as the pieces left behind prove.

MYRTLE   An inlay and veneer wood with curly grain pattern, varying in color from light cream to rich brown.

OAK   A medium-amber wood, tough, hard-wearing, but not easy to work or carve, which was the basic raw material of the heavy furniture styles of Gothic, Tudor and Jacobean England and the early Renaissance. Oak was largely supplanted in the seventeenth century by the more graceful walnut.

OLIVE   A fine-grained, light yellow-brown wood distinguished by dark wavy lines and mottlings, hence its extensive use for veneers and inlays. As the olive tree was common to and prevalent in the hot-climate countries its use dates back to the Egyptians, Greeks and Romans. During the French Renaissance and English Stuart eras it appeared in inlays, and today we find it in marquetry and such turned accessories as boxes, bowls and candlesticks.

PEAR   A hard, close-grained wood varying in color from a light warm beige to a medium brown. In furniture, it is found mainly in antique French Provincial and English pieces. We use it for veneers, often staining it black in imitation of ebony.

PECAN   A type of hickory with a warm brown color and a grain that resembles walnut. A native wood in good supply, it is made into much of our commercially produced furniture.

PINE   A soft, white wood that today is finished in many ways, pickled, stained and painted, and provides a raw material for walls, floors and inexpensive furniture and cabinets. Traditionally it is associated with simple country furniture, except in the work of the English cabinetmakers who painted and veneered it. New England pine pieces were usually left in their natural state or darkened with an oil finish.

POPLAR   A pale-yellow soft wood, light in weight, used chiefly for interior parts of furniture or as a core for plywood. Walls in seventeenth-century England were sometimes paneled with poplar.

PRIMAVERA   A white, light, furniture wood, resembling mahogany in texture and characteristics, which is imported from Mexico and Central America.

REDWOOD   The soft red-brown wood of the Pacific Northwest. Its sturdy resistance to decay and insects, and its unique weathering qualities make it ideal for outdoor furniture and house siding. Since it finishes well it has recently been adopted for interior paneling as well.

ROSEWOOD   A richly streaked, dark red-brown wood that takes a high polish. In the eighteenth century, rosewood appeared as a veneer and inlay on costly furniture; in the nineteenth century, as a solid wood, it was made into furniture. We exploit its unusual color and grain for contemporary furniture and as a veneer on plywood wall panels.

SATINWOOD   A light-orange wood with a fine grain, capable of being highly polished. Principally a veneer wood. It marks the changeover from the Georgian solidity of Chippendale to the delicate, classic restraint of Adam and late-Georgian designers.

SYCAMORE   A hard, cross-grained wood that, because of its tendency to warp, is limited to the interior parts of furniture. In England it was dyed grey, dubbed "harewood," and devoted to veneers.

TAMO   A light-yellowish ash from Japan with a grain like oak. When a beautiful veneer is needed for expensive furniture, tamo is one of the first choices.

TEAK   The best-known wood of the Orient, noted for its extreme hardness and resistance to moisture, decay and insects. The color varies from light yellow or straw shade to dark brown with a straight open grain. In our century, teak is identified with Scandinavian furniture.

THUYA   A hard, rich-brown veneer wood with a burly grain, known since the days of the Romans.

TULIPWOOD   A species of rosewood with a deep-tan color and dark-red stripes, which makes both a good solid or veneer wood. Louis XV furniture is often of tulipwood.

TUPELO   A medium-soft, greyish-white gumwood, often stained to imitate mahogany or walnut. Its use is mainly confined to lower-priced furniture, for posts and face veneers.

WALNUT   A leading furniture wood that has held this position since the Renaissance, undoubtedly due to its variety of texture, figure and color—from a light grey-brown to a dark purplish brown—which vary according to the part of the tree it comes from. Considered the most fashionable of woods in the reigns of William and Mary and Queen Anne, it was pushed into the background by mahogany in the eighteenth century, but has been reinstated by contemporary furniture designers such as Jens Risom and Edward Wormley.

YEW   A close-grained red-brown wood that looks like mahogany. An inlay and veneer wood since the seventeenth century, yew is still very much in demand.

ZEBRAWOOD   Dubbed "zebrawood" because of the brown and black stripes on a light-yellow ground that show up when the wood is quartered, this is chiefly used for bandings and inlays although on a large area, such as a veneer on plywood wall paneling, it can be strikingly dramatic.

woodcut   A design cut in intaglio or relief on a block of wood and then impressed on paper or fabric in black or colored inks. Before the days of machine printing most wallpapers and fabrics were patterned by the woodblock technique, but now it mainly survives in the art world.

wood tones   Inclusive term for colors borrowed from those of the various woods—walnut, mahogany, oak, etc.—and reproduced in stains, paints, plastics, fabrics, ceramics.

xanthic colors   Colors with a predominance of yellow, from pale yellow to orange and red.

yarn dyeing   A process in which fibers are dyed before being woven or knitted into fabric.

BIBLIOGRAPHY

Ball, Victoria Kloss. *The Art of Interior Design*
    The Macmillan Co., New York, 1960

Birren, Faber. *Color for Interiors*
    Whitney Library of Design

————. *Principles of Color*
    Van Nostrand Reinhold Co., 1969

————. *Light, Color and Environment*
    Van Nostrand Reinhold Co., 1969

British Colour Council. *Dictionary of Colours for Interior Decoration*
    London, 1949

Burris-Meyer, Elizabeth. *Color and Design in the Decorative Arts*
    Prentice-Hall Inc., New York, 1935

Bustanoby, J. H. *Principles of Color and Color Mixing*
    McGraw-Hill Book Co., New York, 1947

Carpenter, H. B. *Color: A Manual of Its Theory and Practice*
    B. T. Batsford Ltd., London, 1933

Celanese Fibers Marketing Co. *Manmade Fiber & Textile Dictionary*
    Charlotte, N. C., 1965

Chambers, Bernice G. *Color and Design in Apparel*
    Prentice-Hall Inc., New York, 1945

Costantino, Ruth T. *How to Know French Antiques*
    Clarkson N. Potter Inc., New York, 1961

Greer, Michael. *Inside Design*
    Doubleday & Co., Inc., New York, 1962

Halse, Albert O. *The Use of Color in Interiors*
    McGraw-Hill Book Co., New York, 1968

Holmes, J. M. *Color in Interior Decoration*
    The Architectural Press, London, 1931

House & Garden (British). *The Modern Interior*
    St. Martin's Press, New York, 1964

Kornfeld, Albert. *The Doubleday Book of Interior Decorating and Encyclopedia of Styles*
    Doubleday & Co., Inc., New York, 1959

Maerz, A., and Paul, M. Rea. *A Dictionary of Color*
    McGraw-Hill Book Co., New York, 1930

McCall's Decorating Book
    Random House Inc., New York, 1964

Munsell, Albert H. *A Grammar of Color*
    Edited and with foreword by Faber Birren
    Van Nostrand Reinhold Co., New York, 1969

Ostwald, Wilhelm. *The Color Primer*
    Edited and with foreword by Faber Birren
    Van Nostrand Reinhold Co., New York 1969

Plumb, Barbara. *Young Designs in Living*
    The Viking Press, Inc., New York, 1969

Whiton, Sherrill. *Elements of Interior Design and Decoration*
    J. B. Lippincott Co., New York, 1963

Wier, Albert R. *Thesaurus of the Arts*
    G. P. Putnam's Sons, New York, 1943

Wilson, José, and Leaman, Arthur. *Decoration U.S.A.*
    The Macmillan Co., New York, 1965